*The Poetry of Dylan Thomas*

Farewell, who would not wait for a farewell;
Sail the ship that each must sail alone;
Though no man knows if such strange sea-farers
Fare ill or well,
Fare well:

Learn, if you must, what they must learn who sail
The craft that must sink; sail, till the tall cloud
Is closer to the keel than that far floor,
And to those deepest deeps descend, go down;
Though you fare ill, you yet fare well, to be
King of an empty empire's kingdom come,
Amid the ruins and treasures of that sea;

Learn, if you fare well,
There in the last apocalypse of the waves
What twilights deepen on the drowned man drifting
Atlantiswards, what hues light herons' wings
Aloft in sunset skies when earth is dark,
What unheard chords complete all music's close,
When, fierce as rubies in the vein-dark mine,
The lit blood blazes as the brain goes black;

Last jewel of all the world of light until
The kingdom come of greater light, and death of night, and
    death
Of Death, that shall also die,
When all fare well.

# The Poetry of Dylan Thomas

ELDER OLSON

 THE UNIVERSITY OF CHICAGO PRESS

THE UNIVERSITY OF CHICAGO PRESS, CHICAGO 37

Cambridge University Press, London, N.W. 1, England
University of Toronto Press, Toronto, Canada

# ACKNOWLEDGMENTS

Part of this volume is drawn from lectures I delivered in 1948, while serving as Rockefeller Exchange Professor at the University of Frankfurt am Main; part, from three classroom lectures given at the University of Chicago in the summer of 1953, and subsequently condensed into a paper read before the Philological Society of that university; part, from my review of the *Collected Poems,* which was published in the January, 1954, number of *Poetry: A Magazine of Verse.*

I wish to thank the Editors of *Poetry* for permission to use certain passages of that review and Northwestern University Library for permission to use the bibliography compiled by William H. Huff.

I have many other debts of gratitude: to Mrs. R. S. Crane, who prepared the Index of Poems Cited; to Messrs. T. C. F. Lowry, F. N. Karmatz, and Elmer Borklund, students of mine, who supplied me with books. I am especially grateful to certain of my friends and colleagues from whose erudition and sound counsel I benefited greatly: Mr. John G. Kunstmann, who helped me to establish certain very difficult points; Mr. Theodore Silverstein, who read my manuscript; Mr. Gwin Kolb, who read proof; and Mr. R. S. Crane, who read both manuscript and proof. I hope that in this expression of thanks I have not made them party to the errors from which they were unable to save me.

## TABLE OF CONTENTS

# *1* THE UNIVERSE OF THE EARLY POEMS

Dylan Thomas' first book, *Eighteen Poems*, appeared in 1934 and was followed two years later by *Twenty-five Poems*. The contents and the techniques of the two volumes were similar in many respects; the critical reactions to these volumes, with a few exceptions, were similar also. Critics, favorable or unfavorable, found the poetry difficult, irrational, and undisciplined, but also thought it sufficiently important to demand emphatic comment. H. G. Porteus called the poetry "an unconducted tour of bedlam." Louis MacNeice decided that it was wild but rhythmical drunken speech. Stephen Spender made the categorical pronouncement that it was "just poetic stuff with no beginning or end, or intelligent and intelligible control."

Yet, had the poetry of Thomas been such, indeed had it

been such and nothing more, one may doubt whether it would have been singled out for special notice. By 1934 there could scarcely have been anything remarkable about a writer whose works were irrational and undisciplined. Movements such as dadaism and surrealism had notoriously forsworn reason and discipline as vices, and the spate of works produced by dadaists and surrealists was quite sufficient to drown eighteen poems by a relatively unknown artist. What was remarkable about the poetry of Thomas was that it had its effect even before it was understood, and sometimes even when it was misunderstood. The very minimum of the effect, moreover, left the reader with the impression that a poet with a remarkable sense of language and rhythm was saying something important about subjects of importance; at the very worst, he had somehow botched his statement by his violence and obscurity.

There was a further characteristic which distinguished Thomas' work from that of other poets. It was unclassifiable. Its "themes," in so far as they could be grasped at all, were the age-old ones of birth, sex, and death, but they were conceived and treated in a way that was anything but familiar. In an age which was beginning to discuss myth and symbol as universalizing all human experience, this poetry used myth so private and symbol so special that it had the effect of recording unique experiences. The age was beginning to demand that poetry have social reference; the poetry of Thomas, quite obviously, had no social reference. The age was acquiring the habit of considering and judging poetry in terms of the tradition that had given rise to it; the poetry of Thomas was apparently unrelated to any tradition. The age was fond of explicating obscure poetry; the poetry of Thomas was so obscure that no one could explicate it.

For what was to be done about a poet who wrote lines like these?

> Altarwise by owl-light in the half-way house
> The gentleman lay graveward with his furies;

Abaddon in the hangnail cracked from Adam,
And, from his fork, a dog among the fairies,
The atlas-eater with a jaw for news,
Bit out the mandrake with to-morrow's scream. . . .[1]

Edith Sitwell, in a highly appreciative review,[2] sought to interpret these lines and thereby not merely engaged herself in some controversy but provoked the following reproof from the poet himself:

"Miss Edith Sitwell's analysis . . . of the lines 'The atlas-eater with a jaw for news / Bit out the mandrake with to-morrow's scream' seems to me a bit vague. She says the lines refer to 'the violent speed and the sensation-loving, horror-loving craze of modern life.' She doesn't take the literal meaning: that a world-devouring ghost-creature bit out the horror of to-morrow from a gentleman's loins. A 'jaw for news' is an obvious variation of a 'nose for news,' and means that the mouth of the creature can taste already the horror that has not yet come, or can sense its coming, can thrust its tongue into news that has not yet been made, can savour the enormity of the progeny before the seed stirs, can realize the crumbling of dead flesh before the opening of the womb that delivers that flesh to to-morrow. What is this creature? It's the dog among the fairies, the rip and cur among the myths, the snapper at demons, the scarer of ghosts, the wizard's heel-chaser. This poem is a particular incident in a particular adventure, not a general, elliptical deprecation of this 'horrible, crazy, speed-life.' "[3]

How seriously, one may well ask, are we to take the poet's insistence—an oft-repeated one—that his poetry be read literally? If his interpretation of these lines is a literal one, as it presumably is, how literal is it; and how shall we interpret his interpretation? If it is not literal in the strict sense of the term, in what sense is it so?

If we begin by considering the relation of Thomas' para

phrase to the lines in question, certain things are evident at once. "World-devouring" paraphrases "atlas-eater"; but an atlas is not literally the world. If we are to understand "atlas" as standing for "world," we can do so only by first understanding a geographic atlas as representing the world. Similarly with the adaptation of "a nose for news" into "a jaw for news"; such a jaw becomes a possibility only if we equate "news" with the latest events or happenings, as in fact we do in the conventions of ordinary conversation. So, too, with "mandrake" for "horror"; the mandrake is a horror only in the conventions of witchcraft. In short, the relation of the paraphrase to the verses can be seen only if we observe that Thomas is describing things by reference to other things which, in one convention or another, are their representatives or surrogates.

This is scarcely literal language in the ordinary sense, as the reader can easily assure himself by attempting to determine, after Thomas' "literal" exposition, precisely what the "dog among the fairies" is. Is the diction, then, metaphorical? If we take metaphor as the substitution of names made warrantable by a resemblance between the things signified by the names—that is, as the putting of the name of A for that of B, on the ground that A resembles B, or seems to—we can scarcely suppose that Thomas' lines are metaphorical. An atlas of maps does not much *resemble* the world. A person unacquainted with maps would be quite baffled by one, I think, until he had some instruction in the conventions of cartography.

There is this besides: that in understanding metaphor we perceive the substitution of names by keeping the things themselves, or the ideas of them, entirely distinct. If I speak of a man as "a lion in battle," I do not suppose that a lion is a man or that the idea of a lion is the same as the idea of a man. I simply substitute words, on the ground that the man resembles a lion in certain ways. I keep the idea of man constant, and merely augment certain human attributes to the degree in which a lion is supposed to possess them.

4

A metaphor, then, involves verbal substitution merely, whereas in these lines of Thomas' we have the *idea* of atlas substituted for the *idea* of world because an atlas is a cartographic representation of the world; the use of the word is merely a consequence of a conceptual substitution which has already occurred. In short, we have here, not metaphor, but symbolism.

We must beware at this point. First of all, there is a general tendency in contemporary discussion of art to assume that all art is symbolic. If the point of this is that a few strokes of the painter's brush are not really a cat, but still represent a cat; that a block of granite, chiseled a bit, is not really Venus, but represents Venus; that the tones of Chopin's "B Flat Minor Sonata," as it first bursts upon us, are not themselves agitated, but somehow represent agitation; if this is what is meant, we shall all agree at once—but reserve the right to think the observation a somewhat obvious one. If the point is that art must be symbolic simply because it *must* be symbolic, we may well ask: how do you know until you have looked? Suppose we grant that all art is symbolic; what is the difference between poetry which really *can* be read literally and the poetry of Dylan Thomas? What is the difference between "Tintern Abbey" or the "Ode to a Nightingale" and the portion of Thomas' "Altarwise by owl-light" sonnet just quoted?

One generally finds, moreover, that those who assume that all art is symbolic will assume, as having absolute force, some universal symbolic system, such as that afforded by the Freudian or Jungian psychology. The consequence of such an assumption is that the value or meaning of the symbol is known before the symbol is inspected in its context. There is some warrant for this position, I suppose, in that any attempt to set forth a symbolic system must perforce assign certain values to the symbols under certain conditions; but the view that symbols have a fixed and unconditional value, or even function in all cases as symbols, is expressly disavowed by both Freud and Jung.[4] What is more important, it is contrary to fact.

That it is contrary to fact in the present instance can be seen at once. Thomas "admitted to the influence" of Freud;[5] but the reader who seeks to interpret the symbols of Thomas in terms of Freud is not likely to find the poetry very clear. Such a reader will be gratified, no doubt, to observe that Thomas speaks of "the forest of the loin,"[6] that he frequently connects birth with an emergence from water,[7] and in a few other matters appears to conform to the Freudian symbolic. But the negative instances will quickly diminish that gratification. Whereas, for Freud, fruit symbolizes the female breast and definitely does not symbolize offspring, it is generally a child-symbol for Thomas (as indeed it is in common discourse). Whereas, for Freud, caves, churches, and chapels refer to the female genitalia, Thomas uses caves to signify the innermost recesses of the self, and churches and chapels—particularly sunken ones—to signify lost pristine faiths. Thomas associates ladders and climbing, not with sexual intercourse, but with man's spiritual ascent. The reader who has the Jungian archetypes in mind is likely to fare no better, although the experiences with which Thomas deals are archetypal enough; and, much as Thomas is concerned with the experience of birth, the reader who proceeds in terms of the Rankian theory of the birth-trauma is in an excellent way to miss the whole tendency of the poems; indeed, even to miss Thomas' declared purpose in his art.

It is folly to pretend to interpret what anyone says before you have listened to what he has to say; it is worse folly to declare what a work of art must be before you have observed what it is. If universal symbolic systems had unconditional validity, there would be no problem of interpreting Thomas, or any poet. In Thomas' case his symbols, far from yielding to the easy key of a ready-made symbology, demand close inspection, and ultimately yield their meaning only when the reader, by an act of intuition, recognizes the particular derivation of the symbol.

What, for instance, is the meaning of

The twelve triangles of the cherub wind?[8]

The reader who approaches this with symbolic presuppositions is likely to remain baffled; I will spare you the psychological wildernesses into which he would be led. If, on the other hand, he simply thinks about winds a bit, he is likely to remember the tradition of twelve winds blowing from twelve points of the compass and to recall that ancient maps conventionally represented winds as issuing from a small human head with its puffed-out cheeks blowing furiously. When he realizes further that cherubs are often depicted in old religious pictures as bodiless heads, and that, as shown on a flat map, the winds would describe triangles, he has interpreted the symbol.[9] If he subsequently happens on the following passage in one of Thomas' prose stories, his interpretation is confirmed: "He traced [on the map] with his fingers the lightly drawn triangles of two winds, and the mouths of two cornered cherubs. . . . The cherubs blew harder; wind . . . drove on and on."[10] The symbol has nothing to do with Freud or Jung or whomever; it is taken from cartographic and iconographic convention.

Indeed, the symbolism of Thomas is drawn from a whole variety of sources. It falls under three general heads: (1) natural, (2) conventional, and (3) private. The natural symbolism is of the sort that almost any poet, indeed almost any human being, is likely to employ. Light is a symbol of good or knowledge, dark of evil or ignorance, warmth of life or comfort, cold of death or discomfort, ascent of progress or resurrection, descent of regression or death, and so on. Here, if anywhere, ready-made symbologies might have some force; even so, there is nothing invariable about these symbols in

Thomas, nor are they always symbols. Surely there are such *things* as light, dark, warmth, cold, ascent, and descent!

The conventional symbols depend for interpretation upon knowledge of the conventions of the subject from which they are taken. How numerous the kinds of these are may be seen from the fact that Thomas draws them from cartography, astronomy and the history of astronomy, physics, chemistry, botany, anatomy, mechanics, and in particular such pseudo-sciences as go under the name *occulta*—astrology, alchemy, witchcraft, and black magic, among others; from games and sports; from a mass of myth and legend, including some rather recondite rabbinical materials; as well as from the more usual resources of literature and history.

The private symbolism can best be interpreted by following him from work to work, whether of verse or prose, and observing his habits. One observes, thus, that he tends to use wax as a symbol of dead or mortal flesh, oil as a symbol of life, the sea as a symbol of the source of life, salt as a symbol of genesis in the sea. Scissors or knives are symbols of birth (on the ground that the birth-caul is cut open, the birth-string cut) or of death (on the ground that the thread of life is cut, the branch lopped) and of sexual connection (on the ground of its relation to life and death). He analogizes the anatomy of man to the structure of the universe, too, and sees the human microcosm as an image of the macrocosm, and conversely; and this analogy begets a whole series of symbols. Wounds, one of his most persistent symbols, stand for a number of things: the pain of life, the heart, the navel wound, the sexual parts and the sexual act, Christ, the effects of Time. Tailors are often symbols of what sews man together or sews his shroud or cuts the vital thread. Embalmment, particularly of the Egyptian sort, is a symbol of an obstacle that cannot be overcome, or that can be overcome, in the attempt to resurrect the spirit. In all these private symbols there is undoubtedly a fertile field for psychological inquiry; but the psychologist who wishes to investigate had better be willing, first of all, to find out what Thomas is saying.

But why, the reader may very naturally ask at this point, should Thomas have couched his poetry in symbols so esoteric? Indeed, why should he have used symbols at all? Isn't all this a mere riddling and obscuration? Is it necessary for poetry to be as complex as all that? Does this do anything more than complicate the task of reading?

T. S. Eliot has remarked that this age is a complicated one and therefore requires a poetry which is complicated. I am perfectly willing to let this answer content anyone who can be content with it; but I must admit that I do not see the evidence that our age is more complicated than any other, except on a very foreshortened and simplified view of history, and I am not clear in any case why the complexity of an age should necessitate complexity in poetry. (I should like, by the way, the caveman's view on whether lighting a fire is more complex if one rubs sticks or if one presses a button; Spinoza's, let us say, as to whether philosophy is more complex at present than it was in his day; and so on.)

A second notion, much knocked about in the press of late, that contemporary poets have gone in for obscurantism out of sheer perversity, seems even more trivial. I suspect that no answer which depends on what poetry in general *has* to be, in any given age or out of all relation to time, is worth much. Poetry in general does not *have* to be anything determinate at all, as ought to be clear to anyone aware of the vast variety of good poetry in different forms contrived upon different principles and involving different subjects and devices.

Symbolism itself is merely a device,[11] and a special order of symbolism is merely a special order of device; and there is obviously no necessity that poetry or any other art should employ any one device invariably. Thomas is a symbolist, but not all of his poems are symbolistic; indeed, as he developed he seems to have drawn farther and farther away from the use of symbolism. A device may be well or ill used; whether it is well or ill used depends upon the powers of the device—what the device can do—and upon its being more or less effective than any other device in meeting the particular exigencies of the individual poem.

Since all the arts involve invention, and continually discover new devices or new uses for old devices, it is never possible to make a list exhaustive of all the possible uses of a given device; but we may note that symbolism has several principal powers. First, since symbolism involves the representation of one idea through the medium of another, it can cause us to entertain ideas remote from, or totally outside of, ordinary experience, by the extension of ideas we already possess; thus mystics tend to use symbols in their descriptions of the mystical experience precisely because that experience is an extraordinary one.

Second, since the symbolic concept, the idea which stands for another, is always presented in the form of an image (something which can be either perceived by our senses or imagined), symbols can make immediate and vivid what otherwise would be remote and faint, and thus act powerfully upon our thoughts and emotions. Anyone who has observed the influence of patriotic and religious symbols will be well aware of this particular power of symbolism.

Again, symbols can either focus our attention upon a single aspect of something or cause us to conceive that thing in many aspects simultaneously, and so determine our emotional reactions to it. Death, for example, can be conceived in its benignant or its malignant aspects or both, and produces different emotions as it is differently conceived. The artist who symbolizes it by a smiling shadowy angel presents to us a quite different conceptual aspect, and arouses in us quite different emotions, from those produced by the artist who takes for his symbol the corpse amid all the terrors of the charnel-house. Furthermore, it is possible by the choice of a particular symbol to regulate the degree, as well as determine the kind, of emotional reaction; the artist may, for instance, not only arouse a fear of death by his symbol but arouse greater or less fear by the choice of a symbol more or less dreadful. Finally, we can frequently infer from a given symbol something of the character, beliefs, state of mind, or situation of the person who employed the symbol; we should have little difficulty in inferring, from their different symbols for death, a difference between the pagan Greek and the medieval Christian views of death; and a writer can utilize our tendency to make inferences of this kind, depicting the mood, thought, and character of his personages by letting us see the symbolic processes of their minds.

Other devices—metaphor and simile, particularly—share in these powers; but symbols tend to have much greater range and power. A figure of speech is a figure of speech; whatever it puts before us we tend to contemplate, not as an actuality, but as a manner of speaking. A symbol, on the contrary, exhibits something to us as an actuality, and so affects us more strongly. Metaphor and simile are based upon resemblance only; symbols are based upon many other relations. Tools, instruments, and other agencies often symbolize the art, craft, or process in which they are involved, as pestle and mortar stand for the pharmacist's trade. The product or result may be used, as when the art of the engineer is symbolized by a bastion. Materials or parts, particularly distinctive materials or principal parts, may symbolize the whole produced from them, as when the keystone symbolizes the arch. In all these cases there is no question of resemblance. The cross, for example, is a symbol of Christ, not because it resembled him, but because it was the instrument of his martyrdom and because his martyrdom was the instrument of Christian salvation. Precisely because symbolism rests upon many possible relations, it offers greater difficulty of interpretation, when the symbolic basis is obscure, than metaphor, simile, and other forms of comparison. The latter can be solved by considering what resemblance they are

11

founded on; the interpretation of an obscure symbol is much more complex.

Thomas', or any poet's, use of symbols must be judged in terms of its effectiveness in the individual poem; but his general tendency to use them is accounted for, in part at least, by the quality of his imagination.[12] He has been praised as a poet who dealt with the "major themes" of birth, life, love, and death; but some of the worst poetry in existence has been written on these themes, and there is nothing inherent in them, as themes, which demands any particular poetic treatment, symbolic or otherwise. What is much more to the point, and what is likely to strike his reader first of all, is Thomas' extraordinary imaginative *conception* of these themes. His imagination permits him to enter into areas of experience previously unexplored or to unveil new aspects of perfectly common experiences. Part, indeed, of his obscurity results from the sheer unfamiliarity of the world which he presents to us; like certain mystics, he is often forced into symbol and metaphor simply because there is no familiar way of expressing something in itself so unfamiliar.

His imagination is first of all a strange one, an odd one; he sees things quite differently from the way in which we should. We should see flowers on a grave; he sees the dead "who periscope through flowers to the sky."[13] We should see the towering flames after a fire raid; he sees "the fire-dwarfed street."[14] We should see geese high in the air; he sees "geese nearly in heaven."[15] He looks into what we should find opaque, looks down at something we are wont to look up at, looks up where we should look down, peers in where we should peer out, and out where we should look in.

His poetic imagination has its limits, but within those it has enormous range and power—so enormous that we are apt to think of it as unlimited. It transports him instantly into the mysteries of the womb; it informs him how the child feels at the moment of birth, how the fetus feels during its process of development, how the seed feels at the moment of conception, how all would feel and think if they were prescient of the whole of life. Death is no terminus for him; he descends into the grave and suffers the strange and secret existence of the dead, suffers the resolution of the body into its elements and the transmutation of those elements into other forms of life. He can look back on life as only a dead man could, and can rise from the grave in the Resurrection. The Creation and the ultimate Catastrophe are no limits to him; he penetrates into the mind of God before the Creation, and can feel what would be felt by the scattered particles of a universe utterly dissolved. He can be mineral, vegetable, or beast as easily as he can be man; he can penetrate the depths of the earth and the abysses of the sea, and move about in the depths of the unconscious mind as a diver might walk the ocean bottom.

Here, for example, is the Creation:

> In the beginning was the mounting fire
> That set alight the weathers from a spark,
> A three-eyed, red-eyed spark, blunt as a flower;
> Life rose and spouted from the rolling seas,
> Burst in the roots, pumped from the earth and rock
> The secret oils that drive the grass.[16]

Here is the fetus in the womb:

> In the groin of the natural doorway I crouched
>   like a tailor
> Sewing a shroud for a journey. . . .[17]

Here is the child at the moment of birth:

> . . . I rush in a crouch the ghost with a hammer, air. . . .[18]

Here is the mysterious interior geography of the body:

> Dawn breaks behind the eyes;
> From poles of skull and toe the windy blood
> Slides like a sea. . . .[19]

Here we are in the world of the other-than-man:

> My images stalk the trees and the slant sap's tunnel,
> No tread more perilous, the green steps and spire

13

> Mount on man's footfall,
> I with the wooden insect in the tree of nettles,
> In the glass bed of grapes with snail and flower,
> Hearing the weather fall.[20]

Here is one aspect of death:

> All issue armoured, of the grave,
> The red haired cancer still alive,
> The cataracted eyes that filmed their cloth;
> Some dead undid their bushy jaws,
> And bags of blood let out their flies. . . .[21]

Here the Resurrection:

> . . . I shall waken
> To the judge blown bedlam
> Of the uncaged sea bottom
> The cloud climb of the exhaling tomb
> And the bidden dust upsailing
> With his flame in every grain.[22]

These are tokens of a mighty, an appalling imagination that sweeps us up with it, like an angel, and forces us to endure the visions of another world, thronged with enchantments and horrors. This is a great natural force, we cannot be unmoved by it; but there is more than natural genius, there is art; we should not stand so in the immediate presence of strange things, did not Thomas exert every power of image, symbol, and metaphor to transport us there. I have said that the use of a particular device must be judged according to what the device can do in a particular context; we can see something of Thomas' use of symbols, and thereby something of the justification of his symbolic method, by examining an instance of it.

Suppose we take as an example a line from the sonnet quoted at the very beginning of this book: "Abaddon in the hangnail cracked from Adam." The line means that death and perdition were implicit in the flesh since Adam begot it (Abaddon is the Destroying Angel, Death, Apollyon, the Angel of the

Bottomless Pit). A literal statement of the sort I have just made, in interpreting the line, is abstract and produces no particular emotion; one turns it over in one's mind, assents or dissents, and dismisses it. A figure of comparison, such as "Death is implicit in the flesh as if the Destroying Angel himself dwelt in it," would still emphasize the abstraction, and leave the presence of Abaddon as a merely contemplated possibility, something clearly contrary to fact. But the use of the symbol Abaddon (the only symbol in the line, by the way) confronts us immediately, as a matter of horrid fact, with the Destroying Angel lurking as a physical presence within the mortal flesh, and the mortal flesh is his Bottomless Pit; the flesh which the metaphor "hangnail" makes, not the fruit of Adam's loin, but the merest fragment of his flesh, not much alive when torn from him and incapable of further life on its own. (There is a kind of sublimity of the derisive here; for this poet the flesh of all humanity since Adam is nothing but a hangnail.)

Thomas employs symbols in many ways, but here we see his principal use of them: to make immediate and factual what metaphor and analogue would have left remote and fanciful, to coerce the imagination and so coerce belief; he arouses our emotions before we have time to doubt. Through the repeated use of symbols in this fashion, he builds in his first two volumes, as very real indeed, a fantastic universe of his own.

It is a weird and terrible one. Babes, prescient of the agonies of life and death, speak from the womb or, sitting amid its veils and shadows, paint night and day upon its sides. Men brood on maggots which consume their living flesh as they watch. Flesh grows transparent to reveal the winding nerves and veins and the hidden galleries of bones, the worm gnawing at all. Life struggles out of strange seas and disappears into them, or dissolves to dust. The dead, visible in their tombs, display their corrupting limbs, or spy secretly on the living, or rise to seduce dreaming men. The earth is compact of the debris of the charnel; the landscape hints, in its contours, that it is itself a gigantic corpse. Such love as there is, is preparation for horror or is mere addiction; the flesh falls from the beloved to reveal a mummified corpse, the lover knows himself maddened by the devil's-drug of love. There are greater terrors: women with bagpipe breasts, wounded and mutilated men, men in the forms of plants, animals, and burning candles; a giant runner in the form of a grave, who overtakes all who flee him; a mysterious and sinister scissorman and tailor; scissors that stalk about; ships with shrouds for sails; ghosts, who, manacled to the living man, control his actions from subterranean regions; Cadaver, the one corpse hidden in all flesh, who wears living men as his masks; the grave, in the form of a monstrous boxer, whole countries for his hands, who batters men into the tomb; a strange procession of biblical figures, subtly made sinister; serpents, mandrakes, witches, demons, vampires, nameless animals. There are changing weathers and lights in this world, but for the most part there is darkness and gloom, lit only occasionally by dying planets, baleful eyes, or the phosphorescent corruption of the tomb. It is a nightmare universe, a universe of darkness and fright, a world under the "forever falling night" of Time; a world unsaved by Christ, and unsaveable, doomed.

This is the theater of Thomas' early poetry; the reader may ask: Is it not a Grand Guignol theater? Is this not all stage-magic and melodrama?

I think we must distinguish between melodrama and tragedy. It is essential to melodrama, as to the sentimental, romantic, and similar sensational forms,[23] that we should react to the events as events simply, not as events happening to particularized characters. Thus we have, in all such kinds, generalized or "stock" characters who, viewed in terms of their function, are mere circumstances invented to increase the horror, glamor, or pathos already inherent in the event. The plucking-out of eyes, for instance, is horrible, no matter how it happens; it is more horrible if it happens at the hands of a madman; still more horrible if the madman is a gentle soul who fancies he is doing it out of kindness; more horrible still if the act is committed upon an innocent, beautiful, and defenseless girl: such is the genesis of Grand Guignol characters. Not so in tragedy: the tragic figure does not take his character from the event; the event takes on its character from its happening to the tragic figure. When Oedipus plucks out his eyes, the act is a mere token of the fearful grief which has already seized on his soul; we react to the self-mutilation, not as happening to anyone, or to a particular stock figure, but as happening to a man of the stature of Oedipus. In sensational forms character is at a minimum precisely because the emphasis is upon the events; in tragedy character is maximal because not all characters are capable of tragic suffering. The characters of a sensational work have no pre-eminence except in suffering, and except in their suffering are without interest; while the characters of tragedy have no particular pre-eminence in suffering. Countless thousands have suffered more at the hands of their families than Lear, have had more on their consciences than Macbeth, have got into worse jams than Hamlet. The tragic figure is pre-eminent precisely because of his ethical character and because of its consequence for the way in which he suffers.

Moreover, sensational forms have for their end a sensation merely; tragedy arouses the sensation to produce a more complex reaction. In the melodrama, though we fear the event, we want to be there to witness it, and we want it as gory as possible; in tragedy, we suffer with the protagonist, and we desire the tragic catastrophe, in the end, because it is the only way out which is in keeping with his character. There can be no melodrama if we value the characters highly; there can be no tragedy if we do not. Melodrama of the Grand Guignol kind depends upon, and fosters, our taste for the horrible in itself; tragedy, even the kind written by Webster and Tourneur, employs the horrible only because of its relation to a serious view of life.

Doubtless Thomas, like Baudelaire, is at times nothing more than a stage-magician and frights us with fires patently false. But it is naïve to suppose, as Shaw does in his criticism of Shakespeare, that because poetry involves touches that might be effective in melodrama, it is itself melodramatic. The essence of the sensational forms is that they exaggerate and readily depart from truth in order to achieve the sensation they propose; the essence of tragedy is that its action must embody grave and universal truths. The world of the early Thomas is not a melodramatic one because, as symbolic, it presupposes a reference of its horrors to something further, and does not propose them for their own sake; it does not exaggerate, it can barely approximate, the horror of what it symbolizes. Thomas tells us that to a serious and sensitive individual, life in the absence of a sustaining faith is a nightmare, and so it is; that it is the worst of nightmares, and it is; and if that nightmare is as horrible as possible, images which adumbrate that horror do not exaggerate it—they express it. Without their reference, the symbols of Thomas would be melodramatic, even morbid; because they have reference to the serious suffering of a man of some nobility, they are tragic.

# $2$ THE NATURE OF THE POET

Thomas remarked, famously, that his poetry was the record of his individual struggle from darkness to light.[1] The universe of these early symbols is the universe of his darkness; he builds new worlds as he advances in that struggle toward light. It is notable that after the "Altarwise by owl-light" sonnets, he discards nearly all of this particular body of symbols, transforms the remainder, and gradually develops new symbols and new diction to correspond with his changing view of life. In the early poems, Adam is a symbol of sin and of the perishing flesh; in the later, Adam is "upright Adam / [who] Sang upon origin."[2] Eden is at first thought of as the garden where the Apple was eaten; it later becomes associated with the pristine innocence of the earth; the earth is seen as recapturing that innocence at times, in token of the Redemption. The Flood is a terror in the early work; in the later, there is refuge from it in the Ark.

There is always a danger, when a poet's work exhibits some kind of rounding-out and development, that we may tend to treat his poems merely as parts of one long poem. I should like to avoid that danger, but it must be said that Thomas did, after all, achieve some portion of light. If the poetry of the dark period is concerned almost wholly with personal problems, the poetry of the middle phase is charged with powerful and poignant feeling for others—for his wife, his children, his aunt, and the victims of air raids—and the poems of the later volumes are, for the most part, exultant expressions of his faith and love. There are even touches of humor in "Once below a time," the "Author's Prologue," and particularly in "Lament." "Over Sir John's hill" and "Poem on his birthday" contemplate death with calm acceptance; the universe of darkness, with its swarming horrors out of Hieronymous Bosch, has disappeared. He does not move from that Inferno to a Paradiso, but he has recaptured, in the charming natural world of Wales, something of the lost Eden and something of a foretoken of Heaven. There is undoubtedly a development from doubt and fear to faith and hope, and the moving cause is love; he comes to love of God by learning to love man and the world of nature.

If the three periods in his work[3] are distinct in their subject matter, they are even more sharply distinct in their diction and prosody. The language of the first period is so very limited, its vocabulary so very small, that it reminds one of Basic English. Repetition of certain words is so frequent as to suggest obsession with them; indeed, at least one critic, Henry Treece, has thought their frequent use an instance of verbal compulsion.[4] "Fork," "fellow," "half," "vein," "suck," "worm" seem to dot every page; the phrase "death's feather," among others, recurs in poem after poem. When a limited vocabulary is used to designate a multiplicity of things, ambiguity is bound to result, obscurits

and we find Thomas using, or rather exploiting, his key-words in a whole variety of senses. "Fork," for instance, is used in nearly all of its senses as noun or verb. The sentences of this period are generally very short or consist, however prolonged, of short members; the verse itself is short-breathed, very much based on the line-length, and its pulsations are irregular in beat and uneven in strength, as if a heart were to beat violently for a moment, flag, stop altogether, and suddenly resume.

The poems following the "Altarwise by owl-light" sonnets are, generally speaking, characterized by a marked increase in vocabulary and a discarding of some of the old—"fork," I think, is never used again after the first sonnet—as well as by extension of breath through longer and longer grammatical units. In the sonnets the iambic pentameter line, although now used as a unit of construction rather than as a limit, is still very much in evidence; in "A Refusal to Mourn" a single sentence extends into the third stanza; in "Poem in October" most of the very long and complex stanzas consist of a single sentence. As the old symbolism is rejected or transformed, symbols also diminish in number and in frequency of use, and there is increasing employment of metaphor and image.

In the last period terseness is supplanted by verbosity; sentences, clauses, phrases even, become not merely long but tremendously so. Adjective is piled on adjective, masses of words are jammed together to make one compound epithet, until the ordinary reader can scarcely stretch his breath over the long reaches of language. Despite the enchanting imagery, one has the feeling that eloquence is sometimes strained. The early work had presented a multiplicity of ideas and emotions in very small compass; the last poems stretch a single thought or emotion to its utmost limits, and perhaps beyond. Curiously enough, he never achieves lucidity; the obscurity wrought by his early terseness slips into the obscurity wrought by his final verbosity. I must confess, too, that I find him often very noisy; that charming poem, the "Author's Prologue," makes a racket

21

quite beyond any demand of its emotion or thought. The early poems depend upon a technique of isolation, of singling out the essential factors of an experience; the very last depend upon a technique of accumulation. Perhaps he becomes a bit too consciously the bard, overwhelming us with his copiousness of language, his eloquence, booming at us, working upon us too obviously, even exciting himself unnecessarily. I do not think him melodramatic in his early poems; but I confess there is some foundation for supposing him sentimental in his last. It is not that one would rather not have had these poems; one would rather have had them better.

All of this goes back to the kind of poet he essentially is. That can best be seen, I think, by comparing Thomas the poet with Thomas the prose-writer. The poet is great; the prose-writer, despite many evident marks of genius, merely highly competent; but the prose-writer is far more versatile than the poet. The prose-writer assumes many characters, devises many situations, plays upon emotions which range from the serious to the comic. The poet assumes a single character; and, strictly speaking, he is a poet only of the most exalted emotions, the most exalted grief or joy. Call him what you will, tragic poet, bard, poet of sublimity; the point is that his proper character is a lofty, a heroic one. You will look in vain in his poetry for wit, elegance, polish, and all the graces which makes us preserve many a lesser poet—graces which, indeed, can be found in his own prose. You will find anger, but it will be no common anger, but the wrath of Achilles. You will find despair, but it is the despair of Philoctetes. So with everything he feels. Compare "A Refusal to Mourn" or "Ceremony After a Fire Raid" or "After the funeral" with John Crowe Ransom's "Bells for John Whiteside's Daughter" or Walter de la Mare's "Sunk Lyonesse," and it will be manifest to you that Thomas never achieves, indeed never attempts, certain ranges of emotion.

Although he comes through love to his faith, we never see him, in the poems, really thinking how others think or feel;

22

they exist simply as objects of his own emotion. In his poetry he is capable of immense emotion for another; but he cannot stand in another's skin. As we read him, we are shaken by what he feels for another, not by the sufferings and the feelings of that other. Moved by grief for a burned child, nobly and powerfully moved as he is, he does not suffer imaginatively the experience of the child, does not share in it in the least; he sees the pain and the horror from without, and the resolution he reaches is a resolution for him, not for the child.[5] This curiously external view is revealed in one of his least successful poems: the death of a hundred-year-old man provides him matter for a string of fantastic conceits, and the poem is really unintelligible, not because it is particularly obscure, but because the emotion he exhibits is impossible to relate to any emotion that the event, however conceived, conceived if you will from the point of view of a man from Mars, could have aroused in us.[6] I have remarked, indeed argued, that Thomas' imagination could transport him anywhere, through all space and all time; but it is also true that, wherever it takes him, he sees nothing but himself. He can enter into worm and animal, but he will look out through his own eyes. He can create worlds; but he creates his worlds in his own image, and remains the center of his own thought and feeling. He is not a Dante, a Chaucer, a Shakespeare, or a Browning, who stood inside the men they made; he is a Keats, a Byron, a Yeats, or an Eliot.

These two limitations—his restriction to certain ranges of emotion and his restriction to one character—must not be taken too seriously, for they amount to this: that he was a lyric poet of the lofty kind. But also they cannot be disregarded; a poet so restricted must either aim at and achieve the sublime, or he fails. When the conception underlying his poem is a powerful and lofty one, and controls all the devices of his poem, Thomas is magnificent; when the conception is trivial, or when his treatment of it does not sufficiently manifest it, he is utterly

23

disappointing. His art demands great energy of thought and passion and all the accoutrements of the grand style; when the high conception is wanting, energy becomes violence and noise, the tragic passions become the melodramatic or the morbid, ecstasy becomes hysteria, and the high style becomes obscure bombast. When the bard is not the bard, the bardic robes may easily be put off; not so the habitual paraphernalia of his art. When Thomas is not master of his tricks, his tricks master him. Within a given period, his good work and his bad involve the same devices; it is their employment, what they are employed on and what they are employed for, that differs; and it makes all the difference.

Let me explain a little what I mean by the "high conception." How it differs from the bare theme, an example or two may make clear. The "Ballad of the Long-legged Bait," one of his best poems, has as its bare theme the notion that salvation must be won through mortification of the flesh. A common enough notion; but in the fiery imagination of Thomas the process of purification becomes the strange voyage of a lone fisherman; the bait is "A girl alive with his hooks through her lips"; she is "all the wanting flesh his enemy," "Sin who had a woman's shape"; and the quarry sought is no less than all that Time and Death have taken; for, since Sin brought Time and Death into the world, the destruction of Sin will restore all that has been lost. With the death of the girl, the sea gives up its dead; Eden returns, "A garden holding to her hand / With birds and animals"; and the sea disappears, accomplishing the prophecy "And there was no more sea." In the terrible actuality of the voyage we never guess its essential fantasy; "the whole / Of the sea is hilly with whales," "All the fishes were rayed in blood," and most beautifully:

> He saw the storm smoke out to kill
> With fuming bows and ram of ice,
> Fire on starlight, rake Jesu's stream;
> And nothing shone on the water's face
>
> But the oil and bubble of the moon. . . .[7]

24

Just as in these last lines the storm is given the menace, the fury and power of a kind of supernatural warship, firing "on starlight" and on "Jesu's stream" (the Milky Way) until nothing shines on the water's face "but the oil and bubble of the moon," so the theme of the whole poem is given the emotional power of its legend: the subjugation of sensual desire becomes mysterious and cruel as the sacrifice of the girl, the salvation takes on the beauty and mystery of the resurrection of the dead and of the past from the sea. There is no hyperbole, no exaggeration here; when we comprehend what Thomas has in mind, we see that his conception is merely accurate; that is to say, as accurate as human conception can be.

Similarly, "Fern Hill" and "Poem in October," both luminous with all the weathers of childhood; "A Refusal to Mourn the Death, by Fire, of a Child in London," apprehending the child's death in its relation to the whole universe (all creation is spanned, awesomely, from beginning to end, in the first stanza, and the last carries us back to the "first dead"); the "Altarwise by owl-light" sonnets (surely among the greatest poems of our century)—all of these are founded upon conceptions possible, we feel, only to a man of great imagination and feeling. Sometimes the conception is of the very essence of passion and feeling such as only a towering character could support. Look at these stark and terrible lines from a poem which I think has gone unnoticed:

> Out of the sighs a little comes,
> But not of grief, for I have knocked down that
> Before the agony; the spirit grows,
> Forgets, and cries;
> A little comes, is tasted and found good;
> All could not disappoint;
> There must, be praised, some certainty,
> If not of loving well, then not,
> And that is true after perpetual defeat.[8]

This is the shape and stamp of a despair as deep as falls on Macbeth after the death of his wife.

Compare such magnificent triumphs with this:

> Tell his street on its back he stopped a sun
> And the craters of his eyes grew springshoots and fire
> When all the keys shot from the locks, and rang.[9]

This, it seems to me, is pure trifling. There is no difficulty here, but there is also no imagination. "He stopped a sun"; that is, he stopped a sun-like bomb, and the sun of the dawn also stopped for him. "The craters of his eyes grew springshoots and fire"; that is, the bomb infused all its fires into him so that they came out of his eyes as out of the craters of volcanoes. Perfectly impossible, I should say, and of no importance. We are told later that a "heavenly ambulance drawn by a wound" awaits him and that "a hundred storks" (symbolic of his hundred years) "perch on the sun's right hand." The poet seems to be trying to be triumphant about this death; he fails so utterly that he is almost derisive. The emotion is unclear; the grounds of it are uncertain; there is not a single detail which could not have been imagined by almost anyone in a fanciful mood. We cannot be much moved by the ambulance and the storks, symbolic or otherwise. In fact, we should be much more moved by a newspaper headline; we are more moved by the title of the poem, which sounds like a line from a newspaper ("Among those killed in the dawn raid was a man aged a hundred"), than we are by the poem. The solitary right touch seems to be "all the keys shot from their locks, and rang," for that suggests the power of the blast; but on second thought that doesn't seem right either: suppose the keys were blown from their locks, a blast in which their ringing would be audible wouldn't be much of a blast. Take the keys symbolically, even; they still make no difference.

I am not, I hope the reader will understand, concerned with Thomas' faults; but the very principles which exhibit his genius when he *is* a genius also exhibit his failures when he fails. I am also not trying to legislate; I will merely point out that the principles by which we judge success or failure are the same.

Put it this way. There are no "rules" or "laws" of art. The only necessity by which the artist, as artist, is bound is that imposed upon him by the particular work he seeks to execute. But if he is executing it, as he must, in a particular medium— language, let us say—he can only make it do what language can do. He can discover new possibilities of language and realize them; but they must be possibilities and not impossibilities. If he is representing something dramatically (i.e., on the stage), his work will have to be something that can possibly be represented on the stage. And if he proposes to affect us, his audience, in any way, he will have to invent something that *will* affect us. All this means that through his single commitment the artist has involved himself in a good many more. Bound to one thing, he is at once bound to many; he suffers the restrictions of his medium, of the way in which he proposes to use it, and of the laws of human nature.

Now this last is particularly stringent. Any artist who proposes to produce an effect in a human audience—whatever effect you will, in whatever audience you will—must incorporate in his work causes which will produce that effect. If he wishes to evoke fear or pity, he must set before us objects which are really objects of fear or pity. He may make us pity or fear things that we never did before; but he will first have to persuade us that they are really pitiable or fearful. He may make us cease to fear or pity that which we previously did; but only, however, by first persuading us that it is not really fearful or pitiable. As a matter of fact it does not even matter whether he proposes to affect us or not: if the work incorporates certain causes, it will produce a certain effect, even though the artist did not intend it; if the work does not incorporate certain causes, it will not produce their effect, though the artist desired that effect with all his soul.

Moreover, if the artist offers his work for our approval, or even proposes to execute a work in some way good, he involves himself in questions of value. We need not worry about theories of aesthetic value here; we have only to consider how we *do* evaluate. We value the arts in terms of their effects on us. If we have any sense of art at all, we tend to value entertainment less highly than art, because entertainment produces only a passing pleasure and because, all things being equal, a passing pleasure is less valuable than an enduring one. We evaluate art itself on principles which are really quite simple; that is to say, the system of values by which we measure and evaluate everything else, and the importance of the effect of art in terms of that system of values. Our reflection on the value of the work, so measured, leads to an evaluation of it as a human performance, and our reflection on the value of the human performance leads to an evaluation of the artist.

Thus we respect the poet who observes no more than we do and conceives it no more profoundly than we should, if only he formulates it better than we could; we respect him still more if he does this better than most poets have. We respect still more the poet who observes more than we do, and still more the poet who feels or conceives more than we; and in proportion as the performance surpasses such standards, our respect increases. We range from the slightest esteem to the greatest awe and wonder according as he does surpass such standards; let him fall below them, and our feelings descend as far as utter contempt. We measure performance as against what it seems impossible anyone should have done; against what only the fine artist could have done; against what most artists could do, what most people could do, what anyone could have done, what only a fool would have done.

Particular judgments arrived at through these principles may be incorrect, because the particular work may somehow be misapprehended; the artist may complain of the particular judgment, but he has no appeal against the principles. Not that they are necessarily right; they may very well be wrong; the point is that they are the grounds on which we inevitably judge. The subtlest and the crudest judgments proceed from them.

In "Dawn Raid" Thomas sees and feels less than we should have, perhaps less than anyone should have seen and felt, and so his verbal skill goes for naught. When he *is* Thomas, when he rises to his true stature, he towers indeed. To see that, you have only to ask yourself whether you think much of a birthday as a poetic theme; and then read "Twenty-four years," "Poem in October," and "Poem on his birthday."

# 3 CHARACTER AND ACTION

Thus far we have been examining the more general characteristics of Thomas' art; we may now turn to the more particular question of his poetic practice. This can be treated under three heads: the kinds of activities he represents his poetic character as engaged in; the particular devices, over and above language, through which he shows us that character as so engaged; and his handling of language.

Thomas tends, like most lyric poets, to exhibit a single character acting in a single situation rather than several *interacting* in a single situation. Those famous old ballads, "The Nut-Brown Maid," "Man, Put Thine Old Cloak about Thee," "The Lass of Lochroyan," and "Edward, Edward," all show the interactions of several characters in a given situation; what the poet exhibits is not the uninterrupted activity of a single individual but the interplay among several individuals acting upon and reacting to one another. Poems like Keats' "Ode on Melancholy," Shelley's "Ode to the West Wind," Arnold's "Dover Beach," on the other hand, give us the uninterrupted activity of a single individual. This is not a question of how many people are *present* at the supposed scene of the poem; it is a question of whether the activity shown involves several agencies or one agent only.

We are talking now, let us understand, of the *activity* and not of whether monologue or dialogue is employed. The latter relates to *how* the poet represents, whereas we are considering *what* he represents. Thomas deals with a single agent, but some of his poems are in dialogue form—"I see the boys of summer" and "Find meat on bones," for example—although in the first of these instances he carefully disguises that fact by omitting quotation marks. In such cases dialogue is a device of representation merely. This is obvious if we reflect that such a poem as Browning's "The Bishop Orders His Tomb at St. Praxed's Church" shows us several characters, that is, the Bishop and his "nephews," in interaction, although this is presented through the Bishop's monologue; whereas Thomas' dialogues are merely devices to state two different sides of a case or two different moods, and merely externalize the internal conflict of a single character. The use of dialogue for this purpose is quite common in lyric poetry, and is perfectly distinct from the dialogue of drama. Suppose we call this device "pseudo-drama."

The poet who deals with the uninterrupted activity of a single person in a single situation can do a number of different things besides. He can present an emotional activity merely; show his character feeling joy or melancholy at the change of seasons, grief at separation from his love, and so on. If the poet depicts this sort of activity, we can tell what emotion or desire the character feels, but we cannot state his *moral* condition;

we know what the character feels but not whether he is ethically good or bad.

Consider this example:

### THE LOVER IN WINTER PLAINETH
### FOR THE SPRING

O western wind, when wilt thou blow
That the small rain down can rain?
Christ, that my love were in my arms
And I in my bed again!

This poem is deservedly famous because of its powerful passion; we sense the passion at once and are moved into instant sympathy with it. But, clear as the passion is, we can say nothing of the moral character of the lover. Morality in fact is irrelevant to this sort of poem, for such poems treat of emotions simply, and no one is good or bad simply because he has emotions.

In short, in such poems the person is characterized as having desires of the sort we think of as universal, or as feeling emotions that anyone might feel in his situation. We should neither praise him nor blame him for feeling as he does; we only sympathize with him. The case is very different when the poet exhibits to us a moral activity, shows us the inner workings of a soul which is good or evil; here our emotional reaction to what we see is not based simply upon human sympathy, but upon our moral approval or disapproval of the character. We do not here necessarily sympathize with the feelings of the character; we may quite possibly feel the opposite of what he feels. In Browning's "Soliloquy in a Spanish Cloister," for example, we are shown a character consumed with deadly hatred; far from feeling his hatred, we disapprove of it, and give our affection to the innocent old monk whom he hates.

These two kinds of lyric activity, the merely emotional and the moral, are private, in the sense that they are concerned with thinking and feeling and not with doing. There is an obvious difference between *feeling* such violent hatred as is felt by our man in the Spanish cloister and *acting* on that hatred. A third kind of lyric activity, however, is action itself; the poet shows us his character acting upon someone else, threatening, pleading, commanding, or whatever. Compare the soliloquy just mentioned with Browning's "My Last Duchess," and you will see the difference at once. The fellow in the cloister feels anger, contempt, disgust, delight, and a whole series of emotions in consequence of his hatred; he plots and schemes; but he does not *do* anything. The Duke in "My Last Duchess," however, *is* doing something; he is threatening, and not too subtly either; he is warning the Count's emissary what he expects from his next Duchess; if he should be disappointed, he will be quite prepared to deal with her as he did with his last.

We have, then, three distinct kinds of lyric activity: the simply emotional, the moral but private, and the act itself. Each of these may be matters either of a single moment or of a process; for example, the activity can be that of the character at a single moment of emotion (as in "The Lover in Winter Plaineth for the Spring") or that of the character in an emotional process, over a succession of moments, as in Shelley's "Ode to the West Wind."

Thomas is, as the reader may have guessed, a poet of the internal moral workings of the soul, and he deals, not with moments, but with processes. This is no doubt what he meant when, in one of the few places where he discusses his poetry, he remarked that it was "essentially narrative."[1] But processes are simple or complex, and it is principally the more complex process which engages Thomas. It is not a matter of whether the process is short or long, composed of few stages or many; it is a matter of whether at a given point the process involves a single line of causation or several and, further, whether it involves causes which co-operate or causes which conflict. A man wants a drink of whiskey and takes it; that is a simple process. He hesitates whether to take whiskey or gin and makes up his mind; that is slightly more complex. He hesitates on moral grounds; that is more complex. The more there is in greater conflict, in short, the more complex.

The selection of the dynamic rather than the static, of the complex rather than the simple, has its consequences for poetic method, as Thomas himself was well aware. In a letter to Henry Treece he defends himself against the charge of "diffuseness" as follows:

When you say that I have not [Norman] Cameron's or [Charles] Madge's "concentric movement round a central image," you are not accounting for the fact that it consciously is not my method to move concentrically round a central image. A poem by Cameron *needs* no more than one image; it moves around one idea, from one logical point to another, making a full circle. A poem by myself *needs* a host of images, because its centre is a host of images. I make one image—though "make" is not the word; I let, perhaps, an image be "made" emotionally in me and then apply to it what intellectual and critical forces I possess—let it breed another, let that image contradict the first, make, of the third image bred out of the other two together, a fourth contradictory image, and let them all, within my imposed formal limits, conflict. Each image holds within it the seed of its own destruction, and my dialectal [dialectical?] method, as I understand it, is a constant building up and breaking down of the images that come out of the central seed, which is itself destructive and constructive at the same time.

What I want to try to explain—and it's necessarily vague to me—is that the *life* in any poem of mine cannot move concentrically round a central image; the life must come out of the centre; an image must be born and die in another; and any sequence of my images must be a sequence of creations, recreations, destructions, contradictions. I cannot, either—as Cameron does, and as others do, and this primarily explains his and their writing round the central image—make a poem out of a single motivating experience; I believe in the simple thread of action through a poem, but that is an intellectual thing aimed at lucidity through narrative. My object is, as you say, conventionally "to get things straight." Out of the inevitable conflict of images—inevitable, because of the creative, recreative, destructive and contradictory nature of the motivating centre, the womb of war—I try to make that momentary peace which is a poem. I do not want a poem of mine to be, nor can it be, a circular piece of experience placed nearly outside the living stream of time from which it came; a poem of mine is, or should be, a watertight section of the stream that is flowing all ways, all warring images within it should be reconciled for that small stop of time. I agree that each of my earlier poems might appear to constitute a section from one long poem; that is because I was not successful in making a momentary peace with my images at the correct moment; images were left dangling over the formal limits, and dragged the poem into another; the warring stream ran on over the insecure barriers, the fullstop armistice was pulled and twisted raggedly on into a conflicting series of dots and dashes.[2]

This passage is itself curiously diffuse, curiously confused in its metaphors; but it is not, I think, unclear. The poet who deals with a moment, or even the poet who treats a simple process, can unify his poem in terms of a single image. The poet concerned with a complex process cannot; he must effect unity by "the formal limits" of the poem, and within those formal limits everything is in conflict.

This is true enough, but it will, I believe, be even more convincing if we look into the reasons why it is true. The static or momentary poem is necessarily analytic; it breaks a single moment of experience, to use Thomas' phrase, into its constituent elements; but the experience is still whole and single, a single idea, a single intuition, a single emotional reaction or sensation. As a consequence a single image, metaphor, or symbol may be employed to reintegrate the elements "factored out" by the poet into the whole of which they are parts. An image represents a moment of sensation, metaphor and symbol represent a moment of thought and feeling; all will serve only so long as there is something constant in sensation, thought, or feeling. If sensation, thought, or feeling change, they will serve no longer; and the more radical that change, the more radical will be the change in image, metaphor, or symbol. A process of the soul involves changes of sensation, thought, and feeling, hence changes in the images, symbols, and metaphors which express these.

Thomas' characteristic poems are dialectically complex, in the sense that they balance idea against idea, argument against argument; indeed, his images, symbols, and metaphors are often succinct statements of argument, and the reader who fails to recognize them as such is often in danger of misreading the poem as a whole. Thomas has been romanticized as a primitive, an aboriginal, a hairy wild man out of Wales, the elemental antithesis of the intellectual;[3] I am willing to admire the poetic qualities of this view, but I cannot find any truth in it; the fact is that Thomas' poems usually have rigorous intellectual organization. "I see the boys of summer" has been much admired for its "faery imagery"; that it is a terse and complicated argument about how life ought to be lived seems to have escaped notice.

Poem after poem presents argument, if one sees at all what is being presented. "A process in the weather of the heart" and "Light breaks where no sun shines" work out, with extreme complexity, the relations between man and the external universe; so too, though more simply, does "The force that through the green fuse drives the flower." "When once the twilight locks no longer" is a meditation on the origin of the idea of death, terminating in the decision that life is to be lived vigorously. "My world is pyramid" is a strange meditation on the physical child and "the secret child," and resolves the problem of death in these terms, through the discovery that "the secret child" survives. "I, in my intricate image," even stranger as a poem, is again a meditation on death and resolves the problem in favor of Cadaver; it is Cadaver, the hidden corpse in all flesh, who is "master of man." And so on.

Yet the complexity of Thomas' poems goes far beyond the

matter of complex argument and statement. Their complexity is really due to their presenting three lines, so to speak, at once: the process of conscious thought, the process of the emotions, and the process of the subconscious. Imagine three files of people passing through a narrow corridor and pushing against one another in all directions; you will then have a simplified parallel to a Dylan Thomas poem. I say "simplified" because the conflicts are not as simple as that; there is quite possibly a conflict within the dialectical line, as opinion clashes with opinion, argument with argument; and there can be emotional conflict and subconscious conflict as well.

We may miss this complexity of conflict unless we examine Thomas' words with some closeness. Look at the following remarkable passage:

> This world is half the devil's and my own,
> Daft with the drug that's smoking in a girl
> And curling round the bud that forks her eye.
> An old man's shank one-marrowed with my bone,
> And all the herrings smelling in the sea,
> I sit and watch the worm beneath my nail
> Wearing the quick away.[4]

This occurs in a poem in which he is asking himself whether there is anything worth celebrating in life. In Act III, scene 2, in the most famous of soliloquies, Hamlet decides that, discontented as he is with life, he could be content with death, were it not for one thing: that, if death is sleep, one might have bad dreams even in death; "Ay, there's the rub," the obstacle. For the character speaking in Thomas' poem, there is no one rub; he holds, like the Queen in *Richard II*, that "the world is full of rubs." The real question thus, says he, punning on the word "rub," is whether any of these rubs can tickle one to laughter, even "scratch a laughter from the lung," so that one may momentarily forget his fears. Whatever can tickle one so is worth celebrating, and that alone.

These views are implicit in the poem, and are gloomy

enough. What is explicit is gloomier still: if I could be again an unborn child and be tickled by the friction of birth, I should not fear the apple of sin nor the flood of punishment nor the misery of adolescence. If I were a child and tickled by the process of growth, I should not fear even violent death on the scaffold or in war. If I were tickled by the desires of adolescence, I should not fear the "devil in the loin" of sex, nor the grave. If I were tickled sufficiently by the act of sex, I should not fear the miseries of old age, nor the filth and dangers of debauchery, the "sea of scums." And here we have the stanza just quoted.

The point thus far, we may observe, is that the character *does* fear all these things (a really detailed study of the imagery would show how very bitterly he fears them). Now we learn that he is prey to all of them already. He is madly in love; the very bone of his shank unites him to the old man he must be; the stench of the sea of debauchery is already in his nostrils; death is already gnawing at him in the very pulse of his veins. Notice that whatever he fears, he also desires as much as he fears. What attracts or compels him is also what repels him; he shares his world with the devil.

There is subconscious conflict here, since all the processes of life are associated with sex; sex is desirable, indeed compelling, but it does not sufficiently gratify to shut out fear, and, moreover, it is associated with sin, senile impotency, pain, and death, and so undesirable. Yet, since association is reciprocal, these in turn are desirable, indeed compulsive, since they are linked to sex. Again, there is rational conflict, because he is aware that what attracts him also repels him, and cannot come to terms with himself as to whether what he desires is really desirable or not. He knows, too, that his rational decision will not matter in the end, for he is compelled; at the same time he would like his rational decision to triumph. And there is emotional conflict stemming both from his reason and from his subconscious. The former with its *ought* and *ought-not, can* and *cannot,* balances each of these with its contradictory, and generates emotions based on conflicting moral dictates and conflicting ideas of the possible and impossible. The latter generates emotions of simultaneous hope and fear based on simultaneous desire and aversion; and the emotions generated by the conscious mind also conflict with those generated by the subconscious.

The language of the passage is dreadfully revelatory of all this. He is in love; but see how he puts it. He is "daft," but this is no pretty convention of "love-madness"; he is suffering hallucinations as if he had taken a drug—the "drug that's smoking in a girl." Notice "a girl"—a highly impersonal, possibly even contemptuous, designation of the beloved. He does not see her as beautiful; he sees her anatomically, in terms of "the bud that forks her eye"—the branching veins of her eyeball. "Forks her eye" is a painful image; we are bound to call to mind a sharp prong in connection with the sensitive organ of the eye, and the effect is unpleasant in itself. But there is more than that; in a poet as addicted to puns as the early Thomas, we may look for puns; and there is a suggestion both of the fork of the girl's loin, as visible in her eye, and of the pitchfork of the devil with whom the character shares his world—further attraction and repulsion. The girl herself is not responsible for the attraction; it is "the drug." This curls smoking up through her body, but is not part of her; it comes from the devil; we have the devil's fork and the smoke of hell-fire visible in the eye of the beloved. He is repelled; but in the moment of repulsion at sex, he also dreads the impotency of age, "the old man's shank" already preparing in his groin; at the moment of repulsion at the thought of impotency, he dreads the "sea of scums" and can already smell its stench. What does he do? He sits and watches the vein pulsing below his fingernail; and he sees it as a worm "wearing the quick away," robbing him of life even as its pulse gives him life. And that pulsation is "the only rub that tickles."

The character in this poem—one assumed again and again and constant throughout changing moods and situations—is a modern Hamlet; but, in the old phrase, he out-Hamlets Hamlet. Hamlet's problems stem from a particular situation; Thomas' character has as his problem life itself. He is a simpler character than Hamlet; while he has a grim humor of his own, he lacks Hamlet's mordant wit and cynical gaiety. His imagination, too, is "foul as Vulcan's stithy," but though it has its flights like Hamlet's, it never, in the early poems, rises free of hell-smoke. If he is simpler than Hamlet, his problems are more complex and general than Hamlet's. Hamlet shifts more rapidly from mood to mood, but is actually less indecisive than Thomas' hero. Hamlet never doubts, in his practical syllogisms, the moral major premise, but only the instantial minor; Thomas' character doubts both. Hamlet can at least act on impulse; this character has contradictory impulses.

It is not that he does not make decisions; he makes them repeatedly in the early poems, but we remain unconvinced of their durability, or of the possibility of their realization. In his conviction of their soundness, he proclaims, he exhorts, he even boasts; but there is almost always a subjunctive of wish underlying his indicative of fact:

> I would be tickled by the rub that is:
> Man be my metaphor.[5]

> We shall be fit fellows for a life. . . .[6]

> vision
> Of new man strength, I seek the sun.[7]

> O who is glory in the shapeless maps
> Now make the world of me as I have made
> A merry manshape of your walking circle.[8]

I have suggested before that he is a tragic figure; I do not mean that we see him always at moments of suffering but that he has tragic stature. What gives him that? His moral horrors and aspirations; his hideous, all-penetrating doubts; his painful joy in his transitory convictions; his love of truth and hatred of falsehood and hypocrisy; his willingness to stand by the consequences of any solution he finds for his problems; his terrible sensitivity; and his evident genius, for like Hamlet he shows genius, and that in conflict with itself on the basic issues of life. He comes to his culmination, I think, in the "Altarwise by owl-light" sonnets, and it is here that he finds most satisfactorily a kind of solution—a solution which leads him into his further developments in the succeeding stages of Thomas' poetry.

# *4* TECHNIQUES OF DEPICTION

With this much in mind of *what* Thomas depicts—the feelings and thoughts of what sort of character acting and reacting in what way—we may turn to the question of *how* Thomas depicts, that is, the general devices by which he represents his subjects. I have already touched on one of these devices, the "pseudo-drama." I should perhaps explain the term a little more fully at this point. Pseudo-drama is the use of dialogue to suggest that the action represented is the interplay among several distinct persons, whereas in fact there is no such interplay because the "persons" of the dialogue are not distinct. "The Nut-Brown Maid" shows us the interplay of action between two really distinct persons, the Maid and the "banished man," who turns out to be an earl's son; they are as distinct as Macbeth and Lady Macbeth. But in such poems as the medieval "Debate between Soul and Body" or Elinor Wylie's "This Corruptible," in which Mind, Heart, and Soul discuss, the "interplay" is feigned only; there are not several persons here, but one, for Heart, Mind, Body, Soul, are all one person. Again, pseudo-drama is a use of monologue in which a supposed character (who is really, however, only the object of thought of someone thinking) utters the thoughts of the person thinking of him. Whether dialogue or monologue is employed, characters are assumed as mere masks and made the mouthpieces of the real agents. Crazy Jane and the Bishop, in Yeats' "Words for Music Perhaps," are masks of this kind; so are all the "characters" of Eliot's "The Waste Land" (in fact, he tells us himself in one of his notes that they all resolve into one). To put the whole thing more generally: pseudo-drama is the use of dramatic devices to represent *as if dramatic* an action that is not dramatic. Clearly, thus, there is always some sort of trope underlying it.

Among Thomas' pseudo-dramatic dialogues are "I see the boys of summer," "Find meat on bones," and " 'If my head hurt a hair's foot' "; the "masks" in these are, respectively, "the boys of summer" and the person criticizing them; the father and the son; the unborn child and its mother. Instances of pseudo-dramatic monologue are "Before I knocked," "My world is pyramid," and "When once the twilight locks no longer"; the mask in the first is Jesus, in the second "the secret child," in the third the spirit; but all are mouthpieces of the Thomasian hero, think as he thinks, feel as he feels, and speak in his characteristic idiom, with his distinctive vocabulary and turns of language.

The device of pseudo-drama has many uses; it permits concreteness, immediacy, and vividness where these other-wise would be impossible; it can heighten the contrast between two opposing points of view, or between conflicting motives and desires; it can produce a striking degree of economy as well. To take an example; the underlying idea of " 'If my head hurt a hair's foot' " is as follows: If the unborn child foreknew the birth-pangs of its mother, it would rather die than be born; and if the mother knew that it foreknew, she would tell it that there is no escape, it is its doom to be born and suffer life. This is indirect, abstract, and lifeless if stated in the form of hypothetical propositions; the dialogue form removes the hypothetical element and makes all immediate and vivid.

Thomas also uses pseudo-narrative, the narrative parallel of pseudo-drama. The three principal poems utilizing this device are the "Altarwise by owl-light" sonnets, "A Winter's Tale," and the "Ballad of the Long-legged Bait"; the poet had projected a fourth "In Country Heaven," of which "In the white giant's thigh" is a fragment. In these the characters are also masks for aspects of the underlying lyric character; for instance, the girl in the "Ballad" is a symbolic mask of the fleshly desires of the character.

The effectiveness of these devices lies, as I have just said, in the especially vivid actuality and immediacy which they confer; but they also serve, like representative devices in general, to select those aspects of the lyric activity which are necessary for the effect, to arrange these in the order in which they will have their greatest force (for example, to increase their effect through suspense and the unexpected), to set them in a context which will make them intelligible and probable as well, and to bind them into a whole as effective as possible. The scale on which events and activities are represented is also important to their intelligibility, credibility, and effect, and this, too, is a matter of devices of representation.

An essay of limited length cannot develop these numerous and rather complicated topics; I shall make only one or two observations. The lyric poet does not necessarily represent the whole of the lyric action; just as the novelist and the dramatist may exhibit only a part of their plot, leaving the rest to inference, the poet may present only a part of the lyric action. Conversely, again like novelist and dramatist, he may exhibit more than the activity if this requires for its effect some emotional preparation or information. Finally, he may represent the whole of the activity, and nothing more.

There is nothing invariable about Thomas' procedure in this respect; he begins before, after, and with the beginning of his lyric actions, according to the demands of the individual poem. A few poems, like "Over Sir John's hill," have some sort of introduction; the greater number begin with the activity, or after it has begun. "The force that through the green fuse drives the flower," for instance, starts immediately with the intuition that the forces which create and destroy both man and vegetable are identical, and pursues the consequences of that intuition; "If I were tickled by the rub of love," as I have said, begins after the idea which initiates the lyric action. The choice of one or another of these kinds of beginnings depends upon the amount of emotional preparation, or of information, required for the proper effect.

A fairly constant, and quite peculiar, characteristic of Thomas, however, is his use of what we may call *circumstantial ambiguity*. There is a curious difficulty, as one first approaches his poetry, of determining who is saying what or doing what to whom in what circumstances; and it is this that I refer to. Part of the difficulty, no doubt, is due to the difficult language, but part of it, as certainly, is due to his deliberately minimizing, in some instances even omitting, the ordinary indications which settle such questions. He reminds one of a dramatist who should leave out the title of his play, the indications of place and time, the cast of characters, the assignment of speeches, and all stage directions.

Only fifteen or so of the eighty-nine pieces in the *Collected Poems* carry titles not quoted from the poems themselves. The rest, indeed, usually have as title merely their opening words. (A good many were originally published under the heading "Poem.") This is not precisely overstraining one's self to give the reader information. Yet in a good many instances an appropriate title would have made all the difference between clarity and obscurity, between the reader's comprehending and not comprehending. It would have been easy to find titles which would make apparent, for example, that "Where once the waters of your face" is addressed to a dried sea channel, that "When once the twilight locks no longer" is the Spirit talking of how man came upon the idea of death, that "Light breaks where no sun shines," "Foster the light," and "The force that through the green fuse drives the flower" meditate the relation between man and his universe as one of microcosm and macrocosm.

Similarly "I see the boys of summer" gives none of the conventional indications that it is dialogue; certain other pieces, such as "Do you not father me" and the sonnets, ascribe speeches to speakers like "seaweedy," "the antipodes," and the "fake gentleman in suit of spades" (as a matter of fact these are not even really speeches!), and so on. The ambiguity in representation, as in diction, is not merely deliberate; it is studious.

Why should a poet be thus deliberately difficult? Why should he cultivate ambiguity and concealment? I must admit at the outset that there are certain cases in which Thomas' procedure seems to me without any particular artistic point. He is reported, for instance, to have remarked that "In the white giant's thigh" becomes immediately clear to anyone who happens to know that "the white giant's thigh" is a landmark on a Welsh hill;[1] a reader is perhaps entitled, in instances of this sort, to complain that a matter of such special, indeed local, information, especially if it makes the difference between understanding and not understanding, might have been supplied in a note. But it is possible to be entirely too simple-minded about this. Part of the difficulty of Thomas' poetry stems from the oddity and originality of his imagination; part, as he once acknowledged,[2] from the terrific compression he was trying to achieve; part, no doubt, from a certain wilfulness or, at any rate, from his peculiar habits as a poet. Yet we must not suppose that obscurity can have no artistic purpose, that it is a mere fault of literary composition.

It is a device; and one obvious use of it is to force the reader to give a poem the close attention it requires; properly handled, the cryptic excites curiosity rather than disgust, returns the reader again and again to contemplation of the work until the problems it sets have been resolved. I say "properly handled": what makes the difference between proper and improper handling, between the production of curiosity and the production of disgust, is the value of the work to which attention has been so forcibly directed. The poet who puzzles us to force our attention to a work which is not worth attention is a vain fool, deserves our contempt and will get it; but the poet who tantalizes us in order to make us read more closely, and so understand more perfectly and react more completely to, a piece that is delicately and subtly made is perfectly within his rights. He is entitled to the attention he demands, and he rewards us handsomely at the end, not only with the satisfaction which attends the achievement of something difficult, but also with our increased pleasure in the poem as poem. Obscurity, like clarity, is not a criterion but a device of art; it is folly to praise or condemn a work because it does or does not entail the use of a given device. We have rather to ask what the artist gains or loses by using it or not using it, what he does with it or could have done with it.

But there are other and more important reasons for obscurity or concealment. We can see something of these if we consider how the poet produces emotional effects in us. If we leave aside the sympathetic reactions produced in us by sound and rhythm, we can say, with fair accuracy, that poetry moves us by causing us to entertain opinions. Not every sort of opinion, however; but opinions which have to do with what is a good thing or a bad to do or have happen to one, opinions that such and such a thing is likely or unlikely, impossible or inevitable, immediate or remote; and opinions also which concern the person who does the thing or who has it happen to him—whether we have a favorable opinion of him or not, for instance, and all such matters.

That opinion is so involved in emotion can be seen from the fact that if, for example, we think that something dreadful is about to happen to ourselves or someone we cherish, we shall feel fear, whether the thing is really dreadful and imminent or not; conversely, if we do not think so, we shall not feel fear, regardless of the true case; and so with the other emotions. But opinion itself is not sufficient; the opinion must be actively entertained, that is, present to the mind, not merely in the background; and it must be present to the mind in the form of an image either of the pain and harm to be suffered or of the dangerous agency that may inflict it. For mere ideas and opinions in the abstract do not move us, as experience shows; they must be concretized and made actual in the imagination (or present to sensation) before they have any working power.

It might be said, thus, that the poet controls the emotions of the audience by regulating the amount of knowledge or opinion (concerning the poetic characters and their fortunes) possessed by the audience at any particular moment, and by regulating the imaginative form which such opinion takes. Dramatist, novelist, and even lyric poet through their representations of the activities of their characters deal out information bit by bit. What the audience feels is a function of what it knows at a given point, of the relation of this to what has gone before, and of any inference which can be made on such bases. Of course the particular emotion or emotions felt at a given point are a resultant also of the whole train of precedent emotions; but when these are examined in retrospect they will also be found to vary with the amount of information available at the point of their inception.

An example may make this a little clearer. Suppose I pick up a newspaper and read the headline "Child Missing." If I feel anything, it is a mild concern. Next day I read "Missing Child Still Unfound." My concern deepens. On succeeding days I read "Missing Child Found," and am relieved; "Police Blunder: Child Still Missing," and my concern is renewed; "Child Believed Kidnapped," and my fear grows more definite; "Parents Receive Ransom Note," and I have a modicum of hope; and, in turn, "Child Found Slain," "Tortured before Death," "Slain Immediately after Kidnaping," "Kidnapers Captured," "Kidnapers Joke about Crime," "Kidnapers Executed" —all supply me with different items of information and evoke this or that emotion in me accordingly. If something happens which presents the case more vividly, or in any way makes it more immediate to me, my interest is still more increased, and my emotions will be stronger still; let me see pictures of the bereaved parents, of the child, of the murder room, the instrument of death, the brutal kidnapers, and I shall react proportionately.

Emotions are particularly heightened by suspense and the unexpected. Suspense is not an emotion in itself, as can be seen from the fact that it can attend many contrary emotions, such as fear and hope; it is merely tension resulting from prolonged uncertainty or from prolonged expectation. The unexpected results when we are cast from one emotion to its opposite because what happens is not merely what we did not expect, but the opposite of a firmly established expectation. Anyone who consults experience can see how joy, grief, fear, and hope are increased or decreased according to the elements of expectation or the reverse which they involve. A child's joy in Christmas is heightened by suspense; a mother's anguish is heightened by her uncertainty as to the fate of her child; we break bad news gently to the unfortunate lest they suffer extreme shock; the prisoner is overjoyed at his unexpected acquittal; the grief of relatives is much mitigated if a death has long been accepted as inevitable; and so on. To produce suspense, the dramatist, novelist, and poet make the issue as uncertain as possible, allowing now the one, now the other, of contending possibilities to have the upper hand; or they delay the expected event, feared or hoped for, as long as possible. To produce the unexpected, they establish an expectation as firmly as possible, and then overthrow it.

Thomas is extraordinarily skilful in the techniques of representation. Great art is impossible of exhaustive discussion, and there is no point in trying to be exhaustive; but consider, for example, the "Ballad of the Long-legged Bait." The poem begins abruptly with the start of a voyage. Before two lines are complete, we have a sense that there is something odd about this voyage; it is not the fisherman who takes a last look at the land and bids it goodbye, but the other way round. Another oddity in the second stanza: the boat seems to be moving as fast "as a bird hooking over the sea." In the third, the "looking land" says, "For my sake sail, and never look back." Our curiosity is aroused; we wonder whether these impossibilities result merely from metaphorical statement. The strangeness increases: night falls, the sun is "shipwrecked west on a pearl," and the moon swims "out of its hulk" (if so, it rises in the *west!*). The boat itself sails faster than ever, for "funnels and masts" go by "in a whirl." And then the bait "stalks" out of the sack. Before we have quite recovered from *that*, we are given the fantastic, the frightening picture of a "girl alive with his hooks through her lips" thrown to the sea. A very strange bait indeed.

Bit by bit the tale unfolds. We are ready to pity the girl, but we learn that she "longs among horses and angels" (sea horses and angelfish, we decide), and we learn that she is evidently in a kind of sexual ecstasy, in which all the creatures of the sea join; she dies as a result of this, but any painful emotions we might feel are canceled as we learn that she was "all the wanting flesh" which was the enemy of the fisherman, that she was Susannah and Sheba and Venus and the women sent by the Tempter in erotic dreams, in short, all "Sin, who had a woman's shape"; and so to the magnificent conclusion in which all that was lost through Sin, Time, and Death emerges with the lost continent from the sea; the fisherman comes to his true home at last, Eden, from which like the Prodigal Son he had been absent; and he possesses his heart again (we learn that it was this he had sacrificed in the shape of a girl), now purified of all sensual desire.

As these things are successively disclosed, we move through curiosity, wonder, astonished horror, bewilderment, regret, and resignation to a surprised delight. We are held in constant suspense until the last line of the poem, for until then we do not know what the action is, or who the agents, or what the circumstances. Nor can we foretell the next development of the action; each new turn undercuts our feelings for the events that have gone before, and sets them in a new light. The host of impossibilities incline us to doubt; the furious actuality of the images forbids us to doubt; we are thus inclined to wonder instead. Thomas forces us to bear in mind every point of the tale, if we would avoid utter confusion; but at the moment when we view it as a whole, we see that the tale has a further reference; and that reference resolves all of our problems and confusions.

The *action* of the poem is a meditation, as I have suggested earlier, on the possibility of salvation through mortification of the flesh. It is *represented* by fixing exclusively on the object of thought, that is, the process of that mortification. By rendering that process symbolically in terms of a voyage, and by showing us that voyage through the report of a narrator who does not penetrate into the thought of the fisherman but who has knowledge of the true significance of the events of the voyage, and can consequently correct by his comments and by the emotions he displays, Thomas controls our immediate emotional responses, until, at the termination of his tale, we see what was back of it.

As we consider each element of the representative device, our admiration for Thomas is likely to increase. Why was it right, in this instance, to fix on the object of thought rather than on the thoughts and emotions of the character thinking? Because these latter are inferrable from the object of thought. Why was it proper to render the process of mortification symbolically? Because the symbolic imagery can arouse more powerful emotions, and these more rapidly and economically, than could the literal delineation. Why was it proper to cast the poem into a narrative which begins after the decision of the "fisherman" to mortify "the wanting flesh," and which bars us from the workings of his mind? Because this increases suspense. Why must the narrator know the real significance of the voyage? To heighten, step by step, the conflict between our superficial interpretations until we are at last driven into comprehension.

# 5 TECHNIQUES OF LANGUAGE

The main difficulty in Thomas' poetry is that offered by his diction. We depend upon diction first of all to get at the poem; unless we can grasp its meaning, we can hardly penetrate to character or activity or situation or anything else; and Thomas puts such formidable obstacles in the path of his reader as sometimes to dampen all hope of understanding him.

An obvious way to remove such difficulty would be to supply the reader with a translation or paraphrase of each of the difficult poems. But this has several serious disadvantages. In the first place the reader is likely to take the mere meaning for the poem itself. Again, paraphrase frustrates the poet's purposes by removing all need for intellectual activity on the part of the reader, although precisely that activity is necessary for the effect of the poem. Again, paraphrase leaves the reader quite unaware of the particular verbal techniques of the poet. Finally, it puts a kind of permanent screen of explication, criticism, and analysis between the reader and the poem, whereas all that, once it has done its job, ought to be got out of the way, to let the reader contemplate the poem. It is absurd to start out to read a poet and wind up reading a critic instead; but that is the sort of thing that paraphrase encourages. This book contains a number of paraphrases, for various reasons; but they should in no case be taken as terminating the process of reading the poems; they are merely beginnings. I don't want to give the reader crutches; I want to give him a push.

The best way to help the reader, I think, is to supply him with a list of things that Thomas is likely to do with language; the reader will then know what to look for and how to deal with it when he finds it. I shall leave out the things that Thomas has in common with other poets, and concentrate on devices more or less peculiar to him.

Thomas is fond of words with multiple meanings and multiple syntactic functions. He uses these for various kinds of puns and similar tricks, for achieving simultaneous meanings, and for parody. For example, "My world is pyramid" plays on various meanings of the word "fellow," which can be a noun meaning a person, partner, friend, or companion; an adjective meaning associate, accompanying, etc.; and a verb with similar meanings. Again the sonnets play upon words like "wether," "weather," "rung" (like a bell), "rung" (of a ladder), "which," "witch," where there is similarity of sound only. Sometimes a name is applied to something because of a *concealed* pun; for instance, the name "Gabriel" in the fifth sonnet is applied to a particular figure because of a concealed pun on a card trump and The Last Trump; and Thomas will sometimes carry the matter further in his diction, developing the consequences of the application of the name. In the present instance, for example, the figure is later called "angel" because, if it is Gabriel, it is an angel.

Sometimes he wants simultaneous meanings of a multiple-meaning word; in "A grief ago," the phrase "boxed into love" has simultaneous meanings; as Thomas himself declared, "'boxed' has the coffin and the pug-glove in it."[1] He will mix levels or kinds of language most startlingly, current with archaic, literary with slang and thieves' lingo, either to achieve simultaneous meanings or to make you consider which meaning he intends. For instance, in "Because the pleasure-bird whistles" the term "bum city" means Sodom, which was a bad city and a city where sodomy was practiced, so that we have both the slang and the vulgar meanings of "bum"; while in "To-day, this insect," "air-drawn windmill" does not mean, as we should take it in current language, "drawn by the air," but has its archaic sense of "drawn on the air" (i.e., "imagined," "illusory"), like Macbeth's "air-drawn dagger." Thomas will also effect parody through the use of similar words: "minstrel angles" for "ministering angels," "maid and head" for "maidenhead," "man through macadam" for "man through Adam," "Sodom To-morrow," "God in bed, good and bad."[2] He uses such parodies for many purposes but chiefly to sharpen an antithesis.

He likes to coin words and devise new uses for words. The coined expressions are nearly all compounds, and some are very strange indeed: "grave-gabbing," "mothers-eyed," "scythe-eyed," "skullfoot," "bird-papped," etc. These compounds are based on no one principle; sometimes they merely put together two words in their literal meanings, sometimes they involve metaphor, sometimes they are condensed paraphrases. Thomas will use nouns quite commonly as verbs, for example, "Jacob to the stars" means "climb Jacob's ladder to the stars,"[3] and there are many similar instances of his wrenching a word out of its conventional function.

His metaphors are likely to give a good deal of trouble.

In the first place, he dislikes the obvious kinds and goes in for kinds in which the resemblance is extremely inobvious; sometimes it is a resemblance which is fancied only, and likely to be fancied only by a man in a particular mood or pursuing a particular train of thought. Second, Thomas likes to make the metaphor appear self-contradictory. Third, he likes to mix metaphors, to achieve various special effects through the dissonances they beget. The result is that his metaphors (and, as we shall see shortly, his periphrases), being made as they are out of such materials as the "metaphysical poets" used in their conceits, become enigmas or riddles, since, unlike the metaphysical poets, Thomas does not make explicit the grounds for his fantastic comparisons and analogies. How on earth, the frustrated reader is likely to cry, can anyone "ring the stars," or anything be "a scythe of hairs"?

It will help a good deal if we classify his metaphors. First, there is the apparently self-contradictory metaphor in which the contradiction comes from incomplete statement; either Thomas has given you the missing part already or will come back later and supply it. In "Our eunuch dreams," for instance, we have "one-dimensioned ghosts." "Ghosts" here is itself a metaphor for images on a movie screen; but how are these "one-dimensioned"? Thomas returns to the metaphor in the succeeding section of the poem, in the lines "The photograph is married to the eye, / Grafts on its bride one-sided skins of truth," and we realize that what he meant by "one-dimensioned" is "one-sided"; there is no further side to a photograph or a movie image. The trick here is that he counted on our reading "one-dimensioned" literally, whereas it is a metaphor. He uses this particular trick here to emphasize his point that, while the photograph and the image are half-true, dreams are totally false.

Second, he uses metaphors which deceive you as to what is being analogized to what. This again involves partial statement which has to be filled out with something that went before or comes after. For example, in "When, like a running grave" we have "time tracks you down," one is quite likely to think of time here merely as a hunter tracking, but the last stanza clarifies this; time is also being analogized to a runner on a cinder track who on completion of his course shapes an oval, an "0," a zero standing for the nothingness of death.

Again, Thomas uses what we may call the metaphor of logical consequence. One of his most famous, and supposedly most simple poems, "In my Craft or Sullen Art," contains some five or six of these. "Sullen art" means "so stubborn, unresponsive, refractory, that if it were human one would call it 'sullen.'" "Spindrift pages" means "if Keats was one who wrote in water, my more ephemeral work ought to be called 'spindrift.'" "Ivory stages" means "stages whereon people act falsely, like actors"; it involves an allusion to the Virgilian gates of ivory and of horn through which the false and the true dreams, respectively, come. This sort of metaphor always contains some supposition or allusion from which the meta-phorical term results as a logical consequence; frequently the supposition is a metaphor of Thomas' own. The "angel" for "Gabriel" business mentioned earlier, for instance, comes from a *previous* metaphor, while "ring the stars" derives from a *subsequent* analogy of stars to bells.

Thomas is also fond of a highly composite metaphor in which the parts are unintelligible until we grasp the whole. In "Over Sir John's hill," for instance, the hill is called "just" and the heron is called "holy." "How so?" the reader may ask. These terms derive from Thomas' over-all comparison of the events taking place to a trial and execution; the hill is just because it is a judge, and it is a judge because, like a judge pronouncing the death sentence, it puts on a black cap—in this instance a black cap of jackdaws. The hawk is seen as the hangman executing small birds, and, since he is a hangman, his stoop is seen as a rope (and a fuse is a sort of rope, so his "rope" is called a "fuse"). The heron is the chaplain or priest and so is called "saint" and "holy." Once one gets the whole, the parts are clear. In the same fashion, the opening stanza of "It is the sinner's dust-tongued bell" is likely to mean little or nothing unless the reader realizes that the details add up to a Black Mass being celebrated, with Satan officiating as priest, and that Time is being compared to Satan executing this office. Again, in the "Author's Prologue," the poet compares himself to Noah; he is building the Ark of his poetry and inviting all the creatures of Wales to enter into it and sail with him, safe against the Flood of fear.

He effects metaphor also by his compounds. These do not usually offer much difficulty. "Lamb white days," for instance, means "days innocent as a lamb is white"; "a springful of larks" means "as many larks as you would find in a whole spring"; "apple towns" means the trees in apple orchards; and so on.[4] Sometimes one part of the compound indicates the circumstances under which the other took place; thus "sky blue trades" means "things I busied myself with, as with a trade, under the blue sky," and similarly "the farm at its white trades" means "all the inhabitants of the farm doing their work in the white snow."[5]

He likes various kinds of *implied* or *suggested* metaphor. We had an example of one sort in the lines quoted earlier from the "Ballad of the Long-legged Bait," where the storm was analogized to a supernatural warship, although the warship itself was never mentioned. This sort of metaphor is produced by mentioning attributes of a thing until a kind of rough definition results. Another sort comes from taking a stock phrase and altering part of it to produce an implied analogy, as, for example, "a nose for news" is altered into "a jaw for news," "the stations of the Cross" into "the stations of the breath," "once upon a time" into "once below a time."[6] Thomas' explanation of the first phrase was quoted at the beginning of this book. The second implies that breath, that

is, life, is like the Passion of Christ; the third implies that
if something can exist *in* time, it can also exist *out* of time;
if what exists in time exists once *upon* a time, what does not
yet exist in time can be said to be once *below* a time.

I must warn again that Thomas is quite willing to deceive
the reader as to what is literal and what is metaphorical, and
so set him on a false track. In "Where once the waters of
your face" the reader tends naturally to take "waters" as
metaphorical and "face" as literal, whereas the opposite is
the case.

He uses periphrasis in so many different ways that classifica-
tion is difficult and perhaps pointless; indeed, he writes as if
he were one of the Welsh enigmatic poets of the fourteenth
century. One of his less successful poems, "Because the pleasure-bird whistles," carries this to an extreme that has irritated
many critics. In this poem "Because the pleasure-bird whistles
after the hot wires" means "Because the song-bird sings more
sweetly after being blinded with red-hot wires or needles";
"a drug-white shower of nerves and food" is the long way
around for "snow," snow being conceived both as the "snow"
of cocaine addicts and as manna from heaven. "A wind that
plucked a goose" means "a wind full of snow like goose feathers"; "the wild tongue breaks its tombs" and "the red, wagged
tongue" refer to fire; "bum city," as I said earlier, means
"Sodom"; the "frozen wife" is Lot's wife; so is "the salt person."

Sometimes the periphrasis is organized about a central
metaphor:

> Turn the sea-spindle lateral,
> The grooved land rotating, that the stylus
> > of lightning
> Dazzle this face of voices on the moon-turned table,
> Let the wax disk babble
> Shames and the damp dishonors, the relic scraping.
> These are your years' recorders. The circular
> > world stands still.[7]

Here the earth is compared to a phonograph record (a "face of voices," a "wax disk") which records one's history and plays it back.

Thomas also uses the Anglo-Saxon device of kenning, as in "windwell" for "source of the wind";[8] and he uses an odd form of periphrasis which makes a familiar thing unfamiliar by describing it accurately but in the manner of a primitive definition: thus "shafted disk" for "clock," "bow-and-arrow birds" for "weathercocks."[9]

His syntax is full of pitfalls for the unwary. We have seen already that he tends to use words in other than their conventional functions; but he is also fond of ambiguous reference, false parallelism, ellipsis (particularly of co-ordinating and subordinating connectives), something that we might call "false apposition," and something else that we may call "delayed complement." To take these in turn: in "Half of the fellow father as he doubles / His sea-sucked Adam in the hollow hulk,"[10] what is the grammatical reference of "he"; and what part of speech is "fellow"? In "Oh miracle of fishes! The long dead bite!,"[11] is "bite" verb or noun? (Constant playing upon phrases like "long-legged bait" suggests that it is a noun, whereas it is a verb; an instance of false parallelism.) In "When, like a running grave" there is an ellipsis of "when" from the second and third lines of the first stanza and from the first line of the second stanza, so that the reader is baffled what to put with what. Here is "false apposition":

> I damp the waxlights in your tower dome.
> Joy is the knock of dust, Cadaver's shoot
> Of bud of Adam through his boxy shift,
> Love's twilit nation and the skull of state,
> Sir, is your doom.[12]

The reader tends to read "Love's twilit nation, etc.," as an appositive, whereas it is not. As to the "delayed complement," in the first stanza of "Poem in October" many words intervene between "hearing" and its infinitive object "beckon" and many again between "beckon" and its object "myself."

Thomas deliberately increases such ambiguities by the use or omission of punctuation. For example, in the paragraph above, the exclamation points tend to make us think "Oh miracle of fishes! The long dead bite!" consists of a pair of phrases; in the first three lines of "A Refusal to Mourn," a little hyphenation would have clarified everything, thus: "Never until the mankind-making / Bird-beast- and flower- / Fathering and all-humbling darkness."

Why should a poet do this? I point you back to our earlier discussion of concealment and disclosure, suspense and surprise. But that is argument, and no one can be argued into liking a poem. I will merely say this: that the reader who perseveres will find that Thomas seldom does what he does pointlessly, and usually rewards the effort of interpretation most handsomely.

The reader may have a final question, after this general discussion of Thomas' art: What did a poet, so obviously given to metaphor and symbol in his poetry, mean by saying that he wanted to be read literally?

Obviously he cannot be read literally; to read him so would be either to run headlong into bewilderment or to miss nine-tenths of what he was saying. We can make the mistake of taking him too literally when he says that he wishes to be read literally; his paraphrases, explanations, and commentaries show him to be a man with anything but a literal mind.

What he meant, I should say, is that he wanted to be *read*, not *read into*. It is common practice for critics nowadays, on one hypothesis or another, to impose a host of meanings on poetry which the text itself in no way justifies, sometimes even contradicts. For such hypothesis-ridden critics any poem is merely an occasion for working their favorite automatic apparatus. Any poem means, not what the poet thought he meant, but what the hypothesis dictates that he must have meant. This is worse than an infringement on the freedom of speech; this is dictation of thought and feeling. Let the poet mention the sea, and he must mean the amniotic fluid; let him talk about a garden, and he is of course referring to Paradise; let him describe the pleasure of a warm and comfortable bed, and he must mean that he wants to go back to the womb. This sort of criticism is not only utterly ridiculous but pernicious; it undercuts the very foundations that make the writing and reading of poetry possible or desirable. It removes any incentive on the poet's part because it determines in advance what he shall mean, and because it reduces what he means to what everyone else must mean. It makes reading unnecessary because if the reader has already accepted one of these apparatuses, he knows in advance what the writer is going to say; it makes reading unpleasant, if the reader has not accepted one, because he knows that any interpretation he makes is likely to turn out utterly wrong; legions of bright lads will wave their textbooks and prove that any meaning mere common sense might find is hopelessly absurd.

What Thomas wanted was for the reader to begin with the idea that he *might* be speaking literally; to declare something a symbol or a metaphor only after it was evident that it could not be a literal expression; to find out, in that case, what kind of symbol or metaphor it was; and so go, eventually, *from the text,* to Thomas' meaning. This is the right way to read Thomas, and the right way to read anything; and it is the only right way.

# 6 THE SONNETS

The modern symbolic poet, seldom content with symbols which are the common counters of everyday discourse, usually contrives his own or borrows them from unexpected sources. As a consequence he is quite likely to be misread by the superficial reader. He deliberately baffles superficial reading, therefore, by the use of inconsistency and incongruity. He runs the risk, in so doing, of being excessively obscure, for there is nothing more puzzling to the human mind than contradiction and irrelevancy, and his readers may, in their puzzlement, decide that he is talking nonsense. As long as his symbols are, like the conventional metaphor, based upon relations which are readily perceived, their significance may be fairly clear; but when, like the conceits of the "metaphysical" poets, they are founded upon conjunctions of things that most people would never connect, they may merely bewilder the reader.

The ten "sonnets" of the "Altarwise by owl-light" sequence are the most difficult of Thomas' poems; indeed, it has been doubted that there is much connection between them.[1] Like many other poems of Thomas, they are difficult in their diction, and present other difficulties as well; but their special problems stem from the complexity, rather than the mere fact, of their symbolism.

How complex that symbolism is can be seen from the fact that it involves at least six distinguishable levels, which the poet intricately interrelates:

(1) a level based on the analogy of human life to the span of a year, which permits the use of phenomena of the seasons to represent events of human life, and vice versa;

(2) a level based on an analogy between the sun and man, permitting the attributes of each to stand for those of the other;

(3) a level of Thomas' "private" symbolism;

(4) a level based on ancient myth, principally Greek, representing the fortunes of the sun in terms of the adventures of the sun-hero Hercules;

(5) a level based on relations of the *constellation* Hercules to other constellations and astronomical phenomena; and

(6) a level derived from the Christian interpretation of levels 4 and 5.

The first level presents no difficulty whatsoever. It is what I have earlier called "natural" symbolism; it is based on an analogy which is the source of some of the oldest metaphors we have, and comes down to us through many different literatures. The second also may be considered natural, for it is an easy corollary from the first. We have already made some observations on Thomas' private symbolism[2] and may leave it at that. The remaining levels, however, require some discussion.

Myth is often regarded as evidence merely of the superstitious or naïvely imaginative tendencies of the ancients, but it is also possible to see in it a symbolic formulation of knowledge, scientific or otherwise.[3] The Hercules myths, for example, can be viewed simply as the fantastic adventures of an improbable hero or as evidence of the credulity of the ancients; they can also be seen as a symbolic statement of a not inconsiderable body of astronomical information. According to Plutarch, the "Orphic Hymns," and Porphyry, the twelve labors represent the sun's annual passage through the twelve signs of the zodiac, and Hercules is the sun;[4] and this view has been maintained time and again, and with considerable ingenuity, by later writers. The first adventure, with the Nemean lion, and the twelfth, with the dragon guardian of the Apples of the Hesperides, would indicate, on this view, that the sun thus celebrated is the fierce sun of the summer solstice; but in general cultures seem to have varied the conception of the sun-hero and of his adventures according to their particular interests, agricultural, pastoral, venatic, nautical, or whatever. The Phoenician Melkarth, for example, was a Hercules-figure representing the sun of spring, and was given attributes bearing on commerce, colonization, and agriculture. Nearly all pagan religion involved some sort of solar hero; and thus Thomas treats the myth as summarizing pagan faith.

Whatever stand we may take on the significance of myth, there is no doubt whatsoever that the pagans associated certain constellations with gods, demigods, and heroes. The constellation Virgo, for instance, was Astræa, or Justice; Ceres, Diana of Ephesus, Isis, Atergatis, Cybele, Minerva, Medusa, Erigona, and, in late Roman times, even the Sybil descending, branch in hand, to the infernal regions. Perseus is displayed, sword in one hand, the fatal head of Medusa in the other, daring the sea-monster Cetus, while Andromeda, chained to the rocks, awaits the issue of the battle, together with her father Cepheus and her mother Cassiopeia. Orion, with his dogs, meets the charging bull Taurus. Hercules kneels with one foot on Draco, the Dragon of the Hesperides; he is shown in his culminating triumph.[5]

The appropriation of the heavens, in this fashion, to pagan divinities and myths seems from time to time to have been resented by Christian writers; and, while in general astronomers and astrologists tended to retain the traditional names, there were numerous attempts to Christianize the heavens. A planisphere which Camille Flammarion attributes to Bede[6] converts Aries into St. Peter, Taurus into St. Andrew, and so on. Virgo was easily turned into the Virgin with the Child in her arms; Boötes and Orion were turned into Adam; Perseus became the Angel with the Flaming Sword, Hercules, the Archangel Michael fighting the Dragon; the swan Cygnus became the Cross; Lyra became the Manger, Andromeda the Holy Sepulcher. Eager Christian eyes discerned the Three Magi, Solomon's Seal, David's Chariot, Jacob's staff, Eve, the Serpent, the Tree of Knowledge, and the Tree of Life where pagan eyes had failed to see them; not to mention Job's Coffin, Noah's Ark with its Dove and Raven, and Jonah's Whale. From a depiction of pagan myth, the heavens became an illustrated Bible.[7]

In the "Altarwise" sonnets Thomas plays upon these diverse interpretations of the skies; borrowing his symbols from these astronomical conventions, he works out a meditation on the fate of man, to reach a conclusion which seems to settle the problems of his early poetry. While he uses both the pagan and the Christian interpretations, he is committed to the Christian view from the first. The pagan world is for him a world of death; he sees both Hercules the sun and Hercules the constellation as mortal and, what is more, as in decline and as pursued by "furies." They are precisely in the position of man and, like man, are harassed. The warrant of immortality does not lie with these but with Cygnus. In pagan interpretation Cygnus was the swan killed along with the vulture and the eagle by Hercules; Thomas, in accord with the popular Christian tradition, makes it the Northern Cross; and the fortunes of man and the universe are seen varying as Cygnus rises or sets. Virgo, too, is the Virgin Mary for him. He seems to limit himself, with

few exceptions, to constellations visible from the northern lati-
tudes, and in certain cases to place his own interpretations
upon celestial objects.

Perhaps his interpretations in general can be most succinctly
given in a table which contrasts them with the pagan ones:

| Constellation | Pagan | Thomas' |
|---|---|---|
| Hercules | God-Image | Man-image |
| Draco | Dragon | "Fury" |
| Perseus | Hero | The angel Gabriel |
| Cepheus | King of Ethiopia | "King of spots," Pharaoh |
| Cassiopeia | Wife of Cepheus | "Queen with a shuffled heart," "queen in splints" |
| Andromeda | Daughter of Cepheus | The Holy Sepulcher |
| Scorpius | A scorpion | A "fury" |
| Libra | Scales of Justice | "Scaled sea-sawers" |
| Lyra | Lyre of Orpheus | "Sirens," "bagpipe-breasted ladies" |
| Delphinus | Arion's dolphin | Job's coffin, the tomb, "the tall fish" |
| Aquila | The eagle of Hercules | "Rockbird" |
| Ophiucus | Aesculapius | "Priest" |
| Corona Borealis | Crown | The crown of thorns |
| Hydra | Watersnake | "A climbing grave" |
| Cameleopardus | Giraffe | "Skullfoot," "nettle" (pos- sibly, however, it is not the constellation which is referred to but William Blake's "Polypus," i.e., the black interstellar spaces) |
| Puppis | Stern of Argo Navis | "Time's ship-racked gospel" |
| Gemini | The twins Castor and Pollux | "Sheath-decked jacks" |
| Triangulum | Triangle | "Triangle landscape" (the Pyramids) |
| Crater | The goblet | "Salvation's bottle" |
| Cygnus | The swan of Hercules | "Jesu," the Cross |
| Cetus | Sea monster | "Jonah's Moby" |
| Sagitta | Arrow | Arrow |
| Canis Major | The Great Dog, Cer- berus | "Dog among the fairies," "atlas-eater" (Cerberus) |
| Ara | Altar | Altar |
| Eridanus | A river | "Climbing sea" (the Flood?) |
| The Milky Way | The Milky Way | Milk, mushrooms, food |
| Virgo | Astrea, etc. | The Virgin Mary |
| Aries | Ram, lamb | Ram, lamb, St. Peter |
| Sagittarius | Centaur-archer | "Marrow-ladle" |
| Boötes | Plowman | Adam |

The reader who provides himself with a seasonal star-map or with one of the clever and inexpensive star-wheels now available will be able to follow the ensuing discussion with much greater profit.

After the autumnal equinox ("the half-way house") the constellation Hercules declines to the west, followed by Scorpius (the Scorpion), Draco (the Dragon), and the Serpens Caput (Head of the Serpent in Ophiucus, the Snake Holder); these are his "furies" as he goes "graveward." The sun, which the constellation Hercules represents, is moving southward as the year wears on, in the direction of the constellation Ara, the Altar; hence "altarwise." The time is "owl-light," night, and Hercules has passed the meridian or overhead point. He is mortal, possesses, like the rest of us, destruction and perdition implicit in the flesh derived from Adam.[8] A "dog among the fairies," Cerberus, the symbol of death, with its three heads which can smell out the seed and devour all, a head for each age of man,[9] bites out the seed of his loins. Cerberus is a dog, and the only real thing, for Thomas, among the pagan myths; death is the solid fact amid all our fancies. He guards the Equator; he watches the regions of Tartarus, that is, the realms of death. Death will at last devour the world, and an atlas is a symbolic representation, on maps, of the world; hence he is "the atlas-eater." He has "a jaw for news" because he can smell out the seed. In such a world, ruled by death, tomorrow can bring only horror; hence he bites out "the mandrake" from the fork or loin. The astronomical phenomenon behind this is that as Canis Major, the Greater Dog, rises, the constellation Hercules and the head of Draco set. Hercules is represented, as I said, kneeling upon one knee, with one foot on Draco; thus we have the mandrake (man-dragon, and "drake" is the old word for dragon) bitten out from his fork by the dog. Since the mandrake was thought to shriek on being pulled out, and since it is the seed that has been de-voured, we have "to-morrow's scream." It is now dawn. Her-cules, mortality in his flesh, mortality in his seed, now appears as a ghost or a dream of a ghost; whether it is day or not, it is still the "night of time." He is "penny-eyed," has pennies on his eyes, therefore dead. He identifies himself as the "long world's gentleman," the sun in time; he "shares his bed with Capricorn and Cancer," since these zones mark the limits of the sun's northward and southward motions in the course of a year. I have already remarked that the sun is presented by Thomas as mortal and tormented by furies; his ancestry (i.e., Hercules') is phrased mockingly: he is the "Old cock from nowheres and the heaven's egg."[10] His bones are "unbuttoned to the halfway winds," that is, he is dead, and his bones are at the mercy of the equinoctial gales. He is the "gentleman of wounds"; we have thus both Hercules' agony in the shirt of Nessus, and the wounds we saw inflicted upon him. The phrase "on one leg" is explained by the position of the constellational figure. He scrapes "at my cradle"—Swansea, Wales, from the latitude of which the heavens are seen—in a "walking word." This last phrase means "spoke vividly to me by his motion."[11]

### SONNET II: "DEATH IS ALL METAPHORS"

In this sonnet Thomas is apparently musing, or addressing the sun-symbol. Anything is a metaphor for death, since death is the only reality, and therefore illustrated by all things: the weaning and growth of the child, the apparent passage of the sun through the Milky Way (a kind of weaning by "the planet-ducted pelican of circles"). The pelican was supposed to feed its young, even to reclaim them from death, with its own blood;[12] the universe is thus a pelican, feeding its celestial progeny, the stars, on its own substance; the "weaning" may also refer to the detachment of stars from the generating nebula. The "short spark" is the generating principle, that is, God.[13] God does not exist in time, hence is metaphorically

called "short" (in opposition to the "*long* world's gentleman")
and is prior to all forms, hence to the assumption of shape,
hence "in a shapeless country." The "child" is God's progeny,
whether human infant or planet. "Soon sets alight a long
stick" is of course a reference to Meleager, whose life was
measured by the burning of a stick.

The sun (here addressed as "you") climbs upward (northward) along its spiral (apparent) path about the earth. The
spiral is thus its Jacob's ladder to the stars. The rungs of this
ladder are the vertebrae of the giant serpent-constellation
Hydra, hence "Abaddon" (for Thomas is thinking of the de-
pictions of Abaddon or Apollyon, in Christian iconography, as
a serpent). The poles or "verticals" are the longitudes of earth,
the sphere of Adam. But when the sun completes its climb,
death "the hollow agent" (the marrowless skeleton which still
acts on all life) gives its sinister message. We had been told
that every hair of our heads has been numbered (Matt. 10:30),
that nothing, not a hair, will be lost; we are told, after all our
heavenward effort, that our hairs are roots, that *up* is *down,*
and that our hairs are inconsiderable as the roots of nettles or
feathers; we must weather the seasons and bear Time and the
effects of Time like the hemlocks.

Thus the course of the sun's life and of man's gives token
only of death. All things are mortal and show forth their
mortality from infancy; the ladder of growth and ascent is itself
made of bones, and leads in the end downward to death.

The word "rung" is to be noted, since it is played upon
throughout the sonnets. Again, the pelican metaphor is resolved in the crucifixion, in Sonnet VII, of Christ, one of whose
symbols was the pelican.

### SONNET III: "FIRST THERE WAS THE LAMB"

The sun-Hercules figure now recounts his history in terms of
the constellations, beginning with the birth of the "lamb" after
the winter solstice. The lamb is the young Aries, later to be the

Ram under whose sign spring begins; but before that happens the "three dead seasons" (or winter seasons) of Capricorn, Aquarius, and Pisces must be accomplished. The "climbing grave" in which these signs are fulfilled is the immensely long serpent constellation of Hydra (the Serpent is Death, therefore the grave), which rises in the east under these signs and slowly, mounting almost to the zenith, works westward. As the sun enters Aries, spring begins, and Hydra descends; hence it is "horned down," or rather its tail ("butt") is, for this is last "horned down"; the Ram with its horns has put down the serpent-constellation. Hydra is "tree-tailed" because its tail is slim and upright as a tree, and because it is to remind us of the serpent and the tree in Eden. It is "horned down with skull-foot and the skull of toes"; Thomas interprets the constellation Cameleopardus as a sea nettle, jellyfish, or medusa, the shape of which it resembles more than it does a giraffe. It is thus a cephalopod, "brain-foot" or "skullfoot." A circumpolar constellation, it does not set in the latitude of the British Isles but drops northward from the zenith or overhead point as spring comes on. "Thunderous pavements" refers to the stormy skies of spring; "pavement" was used for sky through which the sun thrusts at the peak of its climb in Sonnet II. "In the garden time" is a reference to the legend that the sun was in Aries at the Creation, hence in the time of the Garden of Eden.[14] We have "the flock of horns" because Taurus follows on Aries, and Capella (the she-goat) and her "kids" are up. Considering that we have the worm (Satan) "mounting" Eve, there is small question that we have a further meaning of cuckoldry, especially since a ram is involved.[15]

The sun wakens like Rip Van Winkle into Time from a timeless sleep—a sleep, however, in the vaults both of the grave and of the sky. The constellations Sagittarius (popularly called the "Milk-Dipper") and Delphinus (popularly called "Job's Coffin") descend into the "vaults" before Capricorn. Hence the sun takes his "marrow-ladle / Out of the wrinkled undertaker's van" (notice the play on Rip Van Winkle) and dips into the "descended bone."[16] The presence of marrow repeatedly, in Thomas' poetry and prose, distinguishes the live bone from the dead; the sun thus draws his very life out of death. As the year continues, Aries rises in the east and mounts southerly almost overhead; in the black winter sky it is now "the black ram," "shuffling of the year" because the sky-changes have produced it, and it is now shuffling with age.[17] The autumnal equinox of the northern hemisphere is the vernal equinox of the southern; thus, if we take the antipodes into account, there are *two* springs a year; and so, according to the antipodes, "twice spring chimed."

The sonnet leaves us at the autumnal equinox. The tone is gloomy. A year has passed, or nearly; spring was brief, summer went unmentioned. We rise from the vaults of death and put on the descended bones of death, and in turn die to provide the marrow of another's life; and there is little comfort in the idea that our autumn is another's spring.

SONNET IV: "WHAT IS THE METRE OF THE DICTIONARY?"

The Hercules narrative is interrupted. The sonnet begins with a series of questions and doubts, questionings of faith which the poet had once addressed to the sky. The form of argument is *reductio ad absurdum.* Is not "the Word made flesh" as unintelligible as saying that the dictionary has meter (or the "short spark" length)? If there is a beginning of *being* which takes shape, what size has it before it takes shape? Suppose there is this—"the short spark"—which generates life; if so, it has sex; if sex, gender; what is its gender? Can there be existence divorced from figure, or soul from body, any more than there can be shadow without a shape which casts it? Soul exists apart from body; is not this as absurd as saying that sound has shape? If sound has shape, what is the "shape of Pharaoh's echo"? These, and other "naggings": the stars disappear, the "burning gentry" of the heavens, or "fire-folk," as

Hopkins put it; which "sixth of wind"—north, south, east, or west, or since these are stars, what updraft or downdraft; or if there are twelve winds and we deal with a hemisphere—which sixth of wind blew them out? (Our "sixth of wind" shows what hair-splittings we can manage when faith is not a matter of life and death.)

Doubtless, the poet (or more strictly, his poetic character) concedes, doubters and skeptics are to those who have faith as hunchbacks are to those who are, in the common phrase, "straight as a poker"; "questions are hunchbacks to the poker marrow." Nevertheless; what of death, the marrowless skeleton, the "bamboo man"? Shall these bones live, can the facts of the boneyard be brought together so as to answer these questions, and so make "straight" a "crooked boy," a hunchback, a doubter?

Very well, the poet had imagined the answer; doubt if you will, be hunchbacked and question; deny if you will, "button your bodice on a hump";[18] make jokes about camel's eyes and needles and the kingdom of heaven; but you will enter that kingdom. Die if you will, but what you think so impossible will in the end save you. You will (in your own terms) be found out in your shroud ("My camel's eyes will needle through the shrowd") in whatever grave; you will be restored to life.

So the poet had once imagined God as speaking through the stars; this was how, in the mirror of his love, the features of the stars had appeared to him, glimpsed for a moment or so, "like stills snapped," as "milky mushrooms," as God's bread, as manna:

> a star of faith, pure as the drifting bread,
> As the food and flames of the snow.[19]

Once the whole heaven was "a bread-sided field" of manna. Once it was near and familiar, near and friendly as any "wall of pictures" of friends and relatives in one's home.

Now it is remote as if the images on the films were thrown by powerful arc lamps upon a distant screen. The screen is "the cutting flood" of space; and the aspect of the stars, now seen in their motions, not stills but moving pictures, is no longer familiar and smiling but menacing and mad.

## SONNET V: "AND FROM THE WINDY WEST"

The constellation Hercules now resumes his narrative. At zenith during summer, he is now driven westward to his setting. After the autumnal equinox, at which Sonnet III had left us, Perseus, a circumpolar constellation in the latitude of the British Isles and hence one which does not set, comes from the *west* (that is, it is actually visible as moving from the west toward the east). Since Perseus comes with the horse Pegasus and holds a deadly weapon in each hand—his sword and the fatal head of Medusa—we have "two-gunned Gabriel" in a short wild-west show. The wild west recalls poker, cards recall trumps, trumps The Last Trump—hence "Gabriel." The constellations of the season are now treated as cards. Cepheus is "king of spots" because he is king of Aethiopia, therefore of blacks; "spots" is spades. He is "trumped up," moved to the meridian, as Perseus advances. Cepheus lies near the arm of Cygnus, the Northern Cross; thus we have "from Jesu's sleeve." Cassiopeia, his queen, is also circumpolar; since she very visibly revolves in her chair, she is the "queen with a shuffled heart." The "sheath-decked jacks" are Gemini, the Twins Castor and Pollux; they were warriors, hence armored, hence "decked in sheaths" (dressed in sheaths) or "sheath-decked." The "fake gentleman in suit of spades" is Hercules, our present narrator; "fake" because he represents the sun, but is not the sun; "in suit of spades" because when he is visible it is dark; "black-tongued" for the same reason. He is "tipsy" because he sets upside-down; "tipsy from salvation's bottle" because Crater the Goblet has preceded him, reversed, in the heavens. Virgo lies between him and Crater; possibly this is why "salvation."

Boötes rises in the east well after midnight as the year draws to a close. It is "Byzantine Adam"—Byzantine because eastern; its late rising accounts for "in the night." The arrow Sagitta goes with Hercules and presumably wounds him; thus "for loss of blood" he fell. The Milky Way lowers with him; hence he "slew his hunger under the milky mushrooms." The "climbing sea" is Eridanus, which ascends in the east (thus "from Asia") on winter evenings; its rise is his decline. "Jonah's Moby," Jonah's Moby Dick, is the Whale or Sea-monster Cetus; Lepus the Hare rises after Cetus, and it would not surprise me much, considering the puns we have had already, to find a pun in "snatched me by the hair."

After the wild-west show and the card game, the symbols and diction have been biblical. We have had Gabriel, Adam, Ishmael, "slew," Jonah and his whale; even "the climbing sea" suggests the Flood, and "snatched me by the hair" brings Absalom to mind. But we move now from a nightmare of the Old Testament to nightmare proper. Gabriel reappears, no longer as a cowboy, but as "the frozen angel / Pin-legged on pole-hills" (Perseus is at the overhead point in the cold sky; "pin-legged" means "having legs long and thin as pins" for Thomas). He is "with a black medusa"—not the Medusa in his hand, but the jellyfish medusa Cameleopardus—"by waste seas" of the northern sky. There the white bear (Ursa Minor, the "snowy Bear" of Chapman, the "shuddering Bear" of Eliot, cold because he lies close to the Pole, in fact his tail-tip is the pole-star Polaris) quotes Virgil. The Bear has moved up the Pleiades (or as the Romans called them, the Vergiliae).

The "sirens singing from our lady's sea-straw" are Lyra, which sets where Virgo had set before. "Sea-straw," "sea-weedy," "the dry Sargasso of the tomb," are all death-symbols for Thomas. The Lyre is unfavorably interpreted as sirens because of the earlier significance in the sonnets of musical sound; compare "rung our weathering changes on the ladder" and "spring twice chimed." The sirens are singing of Time, in which all things die, and luring all to death.

Observe that the Northern Cross thus far appears only as Jesu; there is no reference as yet to the crucified Christ. We are, until Sonnet VII, in a world without the redemption of his crucifixion, and that world is a nightmare of Time and Death; a "night of time" which is merely "Christward." And the Trump which Gabriel "trumps up" is a sinister card: the "Pharaoh" of Sonnet IX and a true "last reckoning."

### SONNET VI: "CARTOON OF SLASHES"

The narrative of Hercules is now terminated, and the poet is speaking. A host of the so-called "watery constellations" have paraded through the skies: Aquarius, Pisces, Delphinus, Capricornus, Piscis Austrinus, Cetus, and Eridanus. Hercules, who has set, is now with the sun; he is "tallow-eyed / By lava's light"; that is, a candle, since it permits us to see, "eyes" us with tallow, and Hercules has the sun's burning "lava" for candle. As a constellation, he is a "cartoon of slashes" on the "tide-traced" (sea-worn by the watery signs) "crater" of the depths of space. He reads "in a book of water," moves through a watery season, that is, one of watery signs. Words, read or spoken, are often equated with motion in Thomas' poetry; compare the "walking word" of Sonnet I, the "rocking alphabet" of VII, the "blown word" of X. The progress through the watery signs is slow; hence "split through the oyster vowels." Since he is thus passing his time in reading, he is using up, "burning," the sea-silence "on a wick of words." The sun is now in Capricorn (which, like Hercules, has set); the other watery constellations have not, but Perseus, Cygnus, and Andromeda are low in the west, and the "sea-eye"—the live eye Algol of Medusa's Head in Perseus—sets; the "fork tongue" of Cameleopardus (a sea nettle for Thomas) is extinguished by the sun, that is, by daybreak.

Hercules is reading by the sun's candle, which is wax; the

poet, himself "manwax," "tallow," reads by a wax candle as mortal as himself; Adam, Earth, is also "reading," has "spelt out the seven seas, an evil index"—completed a solar revolution, an evil sign, since it signifies mortality. All things "read" the book of Time or sing of Time, and Time is death; all things discover their mortality. Lyra, the "bagpipe-breasted ladies," are in "the deadweed"; they provide, not the milk of life, but the music of Time and death.[20] The "deadweed" is the "sea-straw," the "dry Sargasso of the tomb" ( cf. "When once the twilight"). Even the sea, so often connected with life in Thomas' symbolism, is here a Dead Sea; the salt sings also.

The utter horror of this calm, mad despair is, I think, more dreadful than the wild agitation of pursuit in Sonnet V. The "bagpipe-breasted ladies" are as terrifying a conception as any of Hieronymus Bosch; the sun is a candle, man blows out another candle, and the "ladies" extinguish the candle of man, blowing out the bandage which keeps wounded man from bleeding to death.[21]

### SONNET VII: "NOW STAMP THE LORD'S PRAYER"

Cygnus, the Northern Cross, has moved northward and is setting north-northwest; for the first time it is recognized as the Cross. This is the Word; it is this that should be written, this that should be read, not the book of Time. Let all prayer be reduced to the Lord's Prayer, let Gospel and Bible consist simply of this, let all other faiths be stripped away ("strip to this tree"). The "tree" is seen for the moment as a live tree, with leaves and roots; there is "genesis in the root," since it is the beginning of life and of the Bible; since it contains the whole Gospel, it is a tree "Bible-leaved." It is the Word (John 1:1) and the "scarecrow word," religion stripped to its essentials (possibly, too, because as Cygnus rises the Crow or Raven, Corvus, moves to its setting). It is "the alphabet" ("I am Alpha and Omega, the beginning and the end"

[Rev. 1:8]) and a "rocking" one because it is the Tree of Life, rocked by the winds. It is to be read by "one light," not the many lights of different sects. Doom on those who deny what it says. Lyra ("my ladies with the teats of music," i.e., the bagpipe-breasted ladies) and Libra, "the scaled sea-sawers," offer Time only; not the nourishment of milk which makes marrow, but a sponge, such as was offered to Christ on the Cross, to draw him out of life. Thus they draw the "bell-voiced" earth, which "chimes" its seasons, out of life, out of "Time, milk, and magic," and that "from the world beginning." Observe that Time, the only tune to which they lend themselves, grows out of their heartbreak, and breaks the heart of all else. Time from the beginning had stalked all things that came into existence—that took "shape" by their very motion and growth (for that too had the "sound" of its "chiming" seasons); Time still "tracks the sound of shape" of everything, man or cloud, in earth or heaven. Time leaves *its* shape, with its mortal sound ("ringing handprint"), on "rose and icicle"; that is, upon the beings of all seasons, whether summer or winter. (Libra, the Scales, appears here in a very unfavorable light, probably because constancy to the Word is the chief subject of the sonnet, whereas Scales suggest vacillation, see-sawing.)[22]

The Cross alone stands, the Word, the sound of life; Time's tune is death, and the poet in his faith rejects it.

### SONNET VIII: "THIS WAS THE CRUCIFIXION"

But the Cross Cygnus goes down like all else. This is the true crucifixion "on the mountain," for it occurs in the heights of the sky; and the "gallow grave," the depths of space, is as bloody as the thorns about Christ's head, for which the poet weeps. If the Cross also must go down, all existence is one wound, a mortal one; life itself is a deathblow, the world is a wound; all life, the poet with it, is crucified in this crucifixion. After Cygnus sets, Virgo, the Virgin, "God's Mary," rises in the east; the constellation appears "bent like three trees." The reference to the three crosses of the crucifixion is obvious, but the comparison is also an accurate image of the constellation. Virgo is "bird-papped" to differentiate her from the "ladies with the teats of music," and also, doubtless, because a bird-sign, Corvus, is with her. Virgo contains patches of interstellar fog; perhaps this is one meaning of "shift," but surely there is a punning reference to her changed position in the heavens. She has "pins for tear-drops" because the stars are like pins—compare "pin-legged" and "pin-hilled" earlier—and this image is painful, like all the others, because the message of the stars, from Sonnet I to IX, is painful. "This was the sky," that is, this is what the sky meant—it was not the "bread-sided field" that the poet had thought; there is in it not manna but death. The poet, then, is Christ's fellow in death—hence the familiar "Jack Christ"—and is crucified also. There are no ministering angels—only "minstrel angles" (recall the sense of minstrelsy and song earlier in Sonnets III, V, VI, and VII)—and the nails are "heaven-driven," not in the sense of the divinely appointed, but of what is decreed by the stars, by the nature of the universe.

The Milky Way runs through Cygnus; hence it can be said to issue from the breast of Christ, so that Christ nourishes "the heaven's children" "from pole to pole." But this is a female attribute: hence "unsex," the word being used here precisely as by Lady Macbeth in Act I, scene 5, to indicate, not absolute sexlessness, but the adoption of characteristics or the performance of actions impossible to a given sex.

The use of "rainbow" here for the Milky Way is highly significant, for the rainbow had been established as a covenant between God and man, as a promise of safety (Gen. 9: 13–17).[23] That covenant cannot now be kept: Christ perishes, like all else, to nourish what comes after. The poet, also crucified, shares in all this, is also "all glory's sawbones," and also "unsex[es] the skeleton," for if Christ is man, man is Christ, and also "suffer[s] the heaven's children through [his] heart-beat." For all this is merely life out of death and death out of life. "Sawbones" is of course slang for "doctor"; the derisive word parodies the conception of Christ the Healer, Christ the Physician. The term, like the earlier "sea-sawers," conjoins two of the important terms of the poem, "see" (*sea, saw*) and "bones."

This is what is witnessed as the setting constellations pass into the regions of the sun. There is no healing, no redemption, no resurrection; there is only immolation, sacrifice, death. Christ is man, man is Christ; we have nothing more, after our faith, than the "pelican" of the universe.

We are now thrown back upon a Christless, a pagan, world. At the beginning of spring, Hercules again rises in the east; the sun is not powerful, hence is presently called "gentle" in this sonnet. This resurgence of Hercules is a resurrection of a sort; indeed, it is the utmost of pagan resurrection: preservation of the corpse by embalmment and entombment, preservation of the spirit in thought and speech embalmed and entombed in writing; thus preservation "in oil and letter." The Egyptian atmosphere of the sonnet is based upon the presence in the heavens of Cepheus, king of Aethiopia, whom Thomas now treats as "Pharaoh," Cassiopeia, Cepheus' queen, now "the queen in splints," and Ophiucus. Ophiucus, or Serpentarius, is the priest-physician Aesculapius, shown in the heavens as holding a giant serpent; he was identified with the Egyptian Hermes, who, as distinguished from the Greek, was god of medicine. His symbols are the cap and the rod ringed with a serpent; hence the "caps and serpents" of line 6. "Dead Cairo's henna" is quite likely Coma Berenices, now high in the heavens. Calligrapher, physician, embalmer, these provide a resurrection with the bitterness of death; for what is resurrected is nothing but the unwound mummy, the corpse, "death from a bandage." The syntax of lines 7–9 is particularly difficult and ambiguous; apparently the meaning is that, in the rant and pretense of scholars such resurrection is restoration to life, they see "gold on such features" (the gilded mask of the mummy); but the mummy case is simply the glove of the hand of Time (cf. "handprint" in Sonnet VII), the shape preserved is that of Time and death and not of life, and the "linen spirit" (i.e., of such entombment in parchment and mummy cloth) consigns Hercules, and with him all, to "dusts and furies," lays him with "priest and pharoah" in the desert "world in the sand," amid the pyramids of the dead; the pyramids are very happily suggested by "triangle landscape" (compare "My world is pyramid," *Collected Poems*, pp. 35–37).[24]

This "resurrection in the desert" does not even offer release from Time; we can realize the presence of Time here if we recall that at least twice elsewhere Thomas had represented Time as Egyptian:

> time, the quiet gentleman
> Whose beard wags in Egyptian wind.[25]

Consider now the old effigy of time, his long beard whitened by an Egyptian sun, his bare feet watered by the Sargasso sea.[26]

The sun and the world are thus to be laid to rest, with the stones of their wandering (the debris of the stars) for their funeral emblems; and the poet with them, the moving debris of death about his neck. The circuits of the stars are meaningless; there is no resurrection, and no escape from death and Time.

### SONNET X: "LET THE TALE'S SAILOR FROM A CHRISTIAN VOYAGE"

The faith that pinned itself to the Cross had failed when the Cross set. But now, says the poet, let the "tale's sailor"— one who has followed the tale, not as an odyssey, a pagan wandering, but as a "Christian voyage"—observe something further. Let him, first, hold the celestial sphere, like Atlas holding up the heavens, and "hold halfway off the dummy bay / Time's ship-racked gospel." This is a bit complicated. I read "dummy bay" (i.e., a dummy of the heaven which is the harbor of a Christian voyager) and "globe" to mean, quite literally, a celestial sphere. The "tale's sailor" is to look "halfway off"—half the circular distance away from—"Time's ship-racked gospel." Now, the constellation Puppis is the stern of the wrecked[27] ship Argo of Jason; near it lie Pyxis, Compass of the Ship, Vela, the Sail, and Carina, the Keel. Horologium, the Clock, lies near these; reference to it would give added point, but I hesitate because it was somewhat recently so named.[28]

If we look "halfway off" Puppis, we see Cygnus about to rise again; it comes up north-northeast about the first of May.[29] At least one of the "rockbirds" is Aquila, the Eagle, bird of the rocks;[30] if we look "through" its eyes (Altair), we look directly at Cygnus, now called "the blown word." Now the heavens are no longer the "world in the sand," or the Dead Sea of Sonnet VI, but a "foam-blue," a living channel imagined by the poet ("seas I image")[31] to float the "tall fish" Delphinus which rises shortly after Cygnus. The thorns of December are now high on the green holly; that is, Corona Borealis rises to the overhead point.

The rainbow is now not the milk of immolation but the covenant which is a "quayrail"—a further guard for those already safe in harbor. The "first Peter" I take as a reference to I Pet. 3:19[32]—this is the passage that offered foundation for the legend of Christ's Harrowing of Hell; if this is right, Christ, then, has descended into the depths only to rescue the spirits prisoned there. Wonder alone is possible: what rhubarb cast into a "foam-blue channel" has sown "a flying garden"? Rhubarb is grown from the old roots; this is an instance, thus, of the "genesis in the root"[33] mentioned in Son-

net VII; not of development of life out of death, but of life
out of life.

Eden is thus restored, "green as beginning": though it "dive"
and disappear, yet it must be restored, with "its two bark
towers";[34] Time may run its course, but what it takes away
it must always restore, until that final Day,[35] when the very
venom of the Serpent builds "our nest of mercies in the rude
red tree." The answering Word has been spelled out in the
stars: "There were a million stars spelling the same word.
And the word of the stars was written clearly upon the sky."[36]

Let us sum up lest the reader remain bewildered after this
long march of constellations. The hero of the poem is a man
who, aware of his sinfulness and mortality, faces the prospect
of death. In Sonnet I, seeing the change of seasons reflected
in the stars themselves, he feels that all nature is mortal; the
very heavens symbolize the transit of all things to death; death
claims the seed before conception, even, because it is mortal
and must exist in time. The true faith, bitter as it is, is in
death; nothing else is real. The sun itself is mortal, he reflects;
and he imagines, or dreams, that the sun speaks to him.

In Sonnet II he muses further. Everything is a metaphor for
death: the growth of the child, the genesis of the planet, the
passage of the sun through the Milky Way; the "short spark"
of God gives life only to light a stick which must be consumed.
The apparent spiral passage of the sun upward (i.e., northward) is in vain, for when the sun reaches the top of the
spiral, it can only descend. The very ladder of ascent is made
of the bones of death, and leads down to death in the end.

In Sonnet III the character imagines the sun as describing
a span of time from the winter solstice to the succeeding
autumnal equinox. A year is short; when it is nearly spent,
there is small comfort in reflecting that our autumn is another's spring. We are born out of death, and other things
are born out of our death; all must die.

In Sonnet IV he realizes that he had once felt otherwise; once he had plagued his faith with questions, played the sophist with it, for at that time he felt secure in his faith; God had him in his care, the stars were manna, he knew nothing of their motion, they were like pictures of friends. Now he sees their motion, and their aspect is sinister.

In Sonnet V he imagines the sun-Hercules narrative as continuing from the autumnal equinox; it is a nightmare in which the stars appear, first as moving-picture cowboys (following the metaphor of movie images in the final lines of Sonnet IV), then as cards, as biblical characters and events, and last as patently nightmare figures. Life is no more than a nightmare dream of death.

In Sonnet VI man and sun are discovered to be like burning candles. Man is wounded with the birth-wound; time will see that he bleeds to death of that wound.

In Sonnet VII the hero of the poem spurns time; nothing is to be gained from time; he pins his faith to the Cross, which he sees in the heavens, sees it as a symbol of God and Christ, as the Tree of Life.

In Sonnet VIII the Cross sets; this is the crucifixion, then, both of Christ and of man; he must die, like Christ, to nourish those who come after. There is no immortality, no redemption, only sacrifice; and he accepts the sacrifice, Christlike. The last line of the sonnet, if you reflect on it, is perhaps the most sublime written in our century.

In Sonnet IX he thinks of the most notable human effort to withstand death: Egyptian embalmment. This preserves the body, to permit the resurrection of a corpse. Writing preserves, similarly, the corpse of the spirit. This, then, is the only resurrection possible; he spurns it; let him be entombed with the dead in a world of death.

In Sonnet X the reappearance of the Cross signalizes the Resurrection to come. His terrors of death had been engendered by the moving heavens; now the heavens, even in their change and motion, spell out the message of God. Let time have its way, then, let the seasons follow on each other, until the Day that will never end, when all will be restored. The passage of days can only bring closer that Day.

The time scheme of the poem is not without its problems. Sonnet VII may possibly refer to the heavens on Christmas Eve, between 8:00 and 9:00 P.M., since Cygnus would then be conspicuous in the west as an upright cross. Sonnets VIII and IX may possibly be descriptions of the skies on the evenings of Good Friday and Holy Saturday, respectively, at the same hours, while the phenomenon described in Sonnet X would be visible before dawn on Easter morning, since Cygnus sets in the very early evening and rises before the sun throughout the period involved.

On this hypothesis the time scheme of the whole poem would appear as follows: Sonnet I covers the night of the autumnal equinox to dawn; Sonnet II follows immediately. Immediately thereafter the sun-figure begins his narrative, recounting his adventures from the winter solstice of two years before to the autumnal equinox of the *preceding* year. The reminiscences of doubt and faith interrupt in Sonnet IV; in Sonnet V the sun narrative is resumed, going to the winter solstice of the preceding year.

At this point, however, we have two possibilities; either there is the actual lapse of time which the celestial descriptions suggest or Thomas' hero is merely turning a celestial globe, and the time lapse is negligible. I cannot settle this point, but I should prefer the latter possibility; "dummy bay," a dummy of the heaven which is our harbor in a "Christian voyage," "the globe I balance," together with the exhortation to hold it as Atlas held up the skies, strongly suggest a celestial globe; and there is the vexed passage earlier, in Sonnet VI, "Adam, time's joker, on a witch of cardboard / Spelt out the seven seas, an evil index," which suggests to me that someone is fooling with time by using some sort of cardboard device, a map, disk, or astral globe of cardboard, which magically accelerates time and which can be made to run backward or forward in time, as can a star disk or globe. If this last is right, the early substitution of "atlas" for "world" is, besides being a symbol, a warning that we are here substituting maps for the real thing.

In any case, we have two "voyages," real or fancied: the Christless one reported in Sonnets III and V, running from winter solstice to winter solstice, and the Christian one from autumnal equinox to the following Easter.

Whatever view be taken, the sonnets are the Apocalypse of the heavens; and, as in Rev. 21:23, the mortal sun is exchanged for the Son: "And the city had no need of the sun, neither of the moon, to shine in it; for the glory of God did lighten it, and the Lamb *is* the light thereof."

Perhaps the reader has now grasped enough of this poem to see its magnificence. A detailed discussion of the subtlety and complexity of Thomas' art in it is matter for a whole book; nevertheless, the very strangeness of the work may keep one from seeing what sort of poem it is.

It is a poem of the same sort as quite familiar ones: "Lycidas," the "Ode on Intimations of Immortality," the "Ode to a Nightingale." It is a meditation on a problem of great seriousness by a character in serious suffering because of that problem. Just as in "Lycidas" the lone "shepherd" invents a fantastic company of figures to assist him in his mourning for his dead friend, imagines their ceremonies over the imaginary effigy of a corpse that never will be recovered from the sea, so Thomas devises the strange legend of the sonnets, to represent the real processes of his hero's mind. The reader is aware of at least one other piece of Thomas' which involves the same device of representation: the "Ballad of the Long-legged Bait"; that poem, however, in its action pursues the consequences of a decision, whereas the sonnets seek and find a decision.

Thomas is symbolic here, as I have said; the question is whether the symbols do not set powerfully and quickly before us the state of mind of the man contemplating. Sonnet I, surely, sets us at once in a gloomy and terrible atmosphere where strange things are happening; we grasp this much before we realize that the gloom and terror come from the contemplation of the sin-ridden mortal flesh, utterly without defense against death. Thomas plays upon symbols and words, but he is not "playing" when he so plays. Look at the fantastic fifth sonnet and ask yourself *why* we go from movie images to cards to biblical characters to sheer nightmare; that is, ask what states of mind these shifts indicate, and you will see that all this is done with a serious purpose. At the close of Sonnet IV the character has reflected on how once the stars were close and friendly as family pictures, glimpsed as "stills"; seen in their motions, they tell another tale, are remote as movie images; if so, they are telling the tritest of all movie stories, the western story; that makes the angel Gabriel (the constellation Perseus) into a cowboy. But Gabriel brings to mind the Last Trump of Doom; the character, as a sinful fellow, had rather not think about that; he converts it instantly into a card trump. The images tell, step by step, a painful story, in which the Heaven he had once hoped for spells out nothing but his doom, until the message is complete, and he realizes that sin, the venom of the Serpent, is to a merciful God nothing but the necessary condition of mercy.

I have sought to make this examination of Thomas as candid as I might, and to see him as truly as possible. I hope I have succeeded in the former; I know I have not succeeded in the latter. The respect which I feel for his poetry has perhaps sometimes led me into eulogy rather than criticism; I can only say that, in my view, to state the facts about his best poems is to eulogize. Conversely, the desire to test him as time will, to try him with the acids which all great poetry must survive, has doubtless at times made me too severe. In the end it does not matter: my errors will be set right. Those of a poet's own age do not have the last word about his value; they do, however, have the first word, and they must realize that there is as much responsibility in uttering the first as in uttering the last, although there is usually small hope that the first will foreshadow the last.

Whether Thomas will survive, whether other times will think him great, depends on no decision of mine; but I believe there are great poems in each of his three periods. I submit that these are, in the first period, "I see the boys of summer," "The force that through the green fuse drives the flower," "If I were tickled by the rub of love," "Especially when the October wind," "Light breaks where no sun shines," "Foster the light," "And death shall have no dominion," and (towering above these, perhaps above all his work) the sonnets we have just examined. Of the second period, which is less rich but contains poems more beautiful than most of the earlier ones, I should propose "A Refusal to Mourn," and "This Side of the Truth." The third period (remember I am speaking, not of time, but of differences in the poems) contains "Poem in October," "A Winter's Tale," "Vision and Prayer," the "Ballad of the Long-legged Bait," and "Fern Hill." If I had to pick the very best of all these, I should conclude for the sonnets, "A Refusal to Mourn," "Vision and Prayer," and the "Ballad": I shall say bluntly that it is inconceivable to me that these should perish, except through sheer mischance.

Besides these I have mentioned, there are many fine poems; as I look over the Table of Contents of the *Collected Poems*, I feel a pang of regret at not having mentioned, for instance, "After the funeral," the "Author's Prologue," and "Ceremony After a Fire Raid." "Do not go gentle into that good night" and "In my Craft or Sullen Art" have been very popular—but I hold them in far less esteem; it would be a pity if they should eclipse the others, I think, for they do not represent the real genius and art of the poet. There are a good many poems that are indifferent, and some that are simply bad; but I have said enough on that score, and, in any case, it is only the good that matters.

Thomas dealt justly with his poetry in writing it, and it is the business of the future to deal as justly with it in judging it; but, whatever the fate of his reputation, this much we who have the first word may say: that he seemed to us one of the great artists of our time, and that, in his struggle from darkness to light, he uncovered darknesses in us that we should otherwise not have known, and brought us to a light we should not otherwise have seen.

*Appendix A*  PROSE PARAPHRASES

The following paraphrases are intended merely to give a general idea of the poems with which they deal, and so to start the reader on the process of reading Thomas.

### 1. "I SEE THE BOYS OF SUMMER"

This poem is a pseudo-drama involving the "boys," their critic, and the poet. The critic speaks first, and charges the boys with seeking ruin; they destroy harvests, freeze the seeds in the soils, are frigid in their loves, and put the Flood before Eden; they destroy the sweetness of summer, entertain thoughts of winter in summer itself, and in the very sunlight think of darkness; the moon also means nothing to them.

Further, if the "boys" take no account of time and season, the summer "children," as yet unborn, make time within the timeless womb, and reckon day and night where these are not. A perverse lot, in short.

The critic predicts that nothing will ever come of such fellows; probably in the winter of their old age they will feel the heat they should have felt in the prime of their summer.

The poet, speaking in the last line, cries out that, if so, they will have preserved youth in their old age.

In Section II the "boys" defend their view: time and the seasons must be challenged, or the very stars are made into bells which chime the hour; to observe time is to be at the mercy of death, night, winter; the old man, watchman of death, does not offer any comforting cry such as "Twelve o'clock and a moony night!"

No, they say, let us be the dark deniers who doubt and deny all; who draw everything out of its opposite; death out of the woman of life, life and love out of dead lovers, light out of the darkness of the sea, straw and not grass out of the planted seed (the reference is to a fertility ritual in which a "womb" is planted to insure the "birth" of vegetation).

We shall reverse everything; elevate the deeps of the sea and lower the high birds, flood the dry deserts with waters, look through gardens for funeral wreaths, celebrate Christmas in spring, and so on.

The poet remarks that the boys promise to include in their experience all the extremes of life.

In the last section the critic says this will end in ruin; there is a time for everything; when man is dead and eaten by maggots, what can he do then? The boys retort that they are young; he responds that no one stays that way; he, for instance, is now what their father was once. The boys refuse to acknowledge any such father; they are the "sons of flint and pitch," the ageless universe.

The poet remarks that the extremes are really one; that in the whole view North Pole and South Pole are the same, "the poles are kissing as they cross." (Thomas uses the same expression in his short story "A Prospect of the Sea" [*Selected Writings*, p. 110], when the hero achieves a universal view of space and time.)

## 2. "OUR EUNUCH DREAMS"

I. Our impotent dreams, useless in daylight, torture our bodies and mate us with the dead; "midnight pulleys" draw to our beds dead girls whose bodies when kissed taste of the shroud.

II. A similar sort of dream; the movie images, which are also ghosts, possessed of seeming life, but which are ghosts visible only in the darkness of the theater, and driven off by day; taken with these illusions, we forget to live ourselves.

III. What is more illusory—these dreams, or the world in which we live at present? Is it better to chase away the shapes of our daylight world, or these "dreams"? The dreams are indeed truer; the photograph is half-true; but our daylight world is like the dreams of Stanza I; in it, too, ghosts obtain life by sucking the marrow (of faith) from living bones.

IV. The present world is worse; a flimsy imitation of the movie, and a dream that makes us honor the dead as if they were alive. Let us have faith, and revolt; cry the ghosts back like a cock, shoot the lying pictures from the films, and we shall not only live well, but be honored by those who come after us.

## 3. "WHEN, LIKE A RUNNING GRAVE"

When time overtakes you (my head and my heart, who have ruled me in life), when what gave one of you peace and the other, love, has a wounding blade for every hair; when love in all her gay apparel is dead, and taken (like a dead turtle-dove) to the dome of the skull (i.e., intellectualized);

When age like a tailor comes to prepare the shroud, then,

release me; I am barer of love than the skull's mouth is of its tongue; barer than the grave, which measures us for our six feet of earth, is bare of concern for our inches of bone;

Deliver me, my masters, head and heart; man, who is merely the candle of the waxen corpse set alight, grows less when each knock of the blood is a push of the spade that digs his grave, and when time brings children into the world as inevitably as bruises to a smashed thumb; deliver me from girls and thoughts of girls, from love both physical and cerebral;

For I, putting on my "best face," willing to be polite, but willing also to fight for what I want (I have "knuckle-dusters" under my "velvet glove"), propose to do something with my life; time and death may well fail to button me in my shroud, using the virgin zero of a void life as a buttonhole;

I shall use this body of mine with all my might, though it is the certain property of death; I stride in all my force, while those who desire intellectual love, those whose very steps tap out in Morse code their despair of physical love and their faith in virginity will end up as eunuchs, with the stains of age, as of acid, on their groins and faces.

Time, you say, is a foolish fancy; no, no; there is a point when time, like an auctioneer ending all bids with a rap of his hammer, puts an end to sex ("honour" has here its obsolete concrete sense of the female sexual organ); when Cadaver from the hangar tells the joy-stick of the plane, "fail" (a sexual allusion again). Love cannot last beyond this, as an intellectual thing, despite the "lover" and "hero" skull.

Sir Head and Madam Heart, joy cannot be felt in (intellectual) images of sex; it does not come from everything that resembles sex; otherwise, the fusion of cancer, the coming-together of feather and tree, the fever of illness, even the pneumatic drill boring through pavement, would all give joy.

I put an end to your hopes, extinguish the tapers you would light (in the dome of the skull) over dead love; the only pleasure is that of dust seeking to beget dust, physical sex, Cadaver begetting new flesh for the grave; when love is a matter of the head, Sir Head, all is over.

Everything ends, tower, the scene of a season, sunlight, flesh, action; realize this, and yield, in due time.

The very wind blowing infects everything with death, like a coughing man; time itself, like a runner on a cinder track, rounds his course and describes a zero; so, reduces all to nothing. Know this, and leave love to Cadaver at the point when you are no longer capable of physical love.

### 4. "FOSTER THE LIGHT"

The poem deals with the poet's desire to be one with the world in which he lives; he will find man in the inhuman universe, if that universe will make him into a world. The poem depends upon the microcosm-macrocosm relation and falls into three parts: the first three stanzas, an exhortation to himself; the fourth stanza, an exhortation to the seas as representing the universe; the final stanza, an exhortation to God:

Extend yourself to be all things; find light wherever there is light, do not obscure the moon; feel all deeply, to the bone, and do not deal with superficialities; make your marrow into an image of the twelve winds of the universe, and let it flow over all like the winds. Acknowledge darkness, too, and master it; do not, like an icicle on a snowman, reduce all the variety of night to one thing, and that not darkness, but its opposite, light.

Celebrate spring, but do not try to hold back the march of seasons; do not crush growth, either of the fanciful or of the real; seek to comprehend all seasons, cultivate summer in winter, winter in summer, live a "vegetable century" in your youth.

Foster all things, even the diabolical (the "fly-lord" is Beëlzebub), but do not live on morbid fancies, a mere parasite of such phantasms; use your magic to feel the world like your own heart within you; let your voice ring out lordly above the "ninnies' choir" of ordinary poetry, utter what the high cloud sings, and make a music even out of horror, bone-deep though it be.

And you, O seas, do not alter your nature; remain inhuman; though I am inconstant and ephemeral, do you not change like a weathercock, but remain fixed in what you are.

God that shaped and colored the seas made me also, and made the ark as a refuge when the flood threatened; O God who is glory without shape or color, make a world of me as I seek humanity in the universe.

## 5. "WHEN ALL MY FIVE AND COUNTRY SENSES SEE"

When all my five native senses can see as clearly as my eyes, touch, that had to do with love and fertility, will see how love ends and is put away like fruit in winter; hearing will see how love is drummed away, how its music ends in discord; the tasting tongue will see how the beloved pains of love are over, and lament; my nostrils will no longer smell, but will see how the very breath of love is consumed as with burning.

But whatever the testimony of all the senses, my heart has better witnesses; these will waken, as the senses themselves fall asleep; though the five senses perish, my heart will develop new senses, remain sensual, and prone to love.

## Appendix B  GLOSSARY

[This glossary is not intended to be complete; it merely offers help on some fifty or so difficult terms. All page references are to the *Collected Poems*.]

AARON (p. 63). Aaron's rod; a plant with a tall stem, such as the great mullein. So called after the rod of Aaron, which miraculously bloomed and bore almonds. See Num. 17:8. The imagery of the poem is chiefly botanical.

ABADDON (p. 80). Apollyon, the Destroying Angel. See Rev. 9:11. In the apocryphal *Evangelium Bartholomei*, Death, in serpent form, with his serpent sons.

ABRAHAM-MAN (p. 54). A beggar feigning madness for the sake of alms; originally, a lunatic from Abraham ward in Bedlam Hospital, the inmates of which were permitted to beg.

ADAM. Used variously; e.g., original man (p. 22); human ("Adam's brine" is salt of the sweat in which man must labor after the

Fall, and salt of the sea which generates man) (p. 34); human form, the image of Adam in his offspring (p. 35); mankind in general (p. 48); Sonnet II, earth (p. 80); Sonnet V, the constellation Boötes (p. 82).

ANIMAL (p. 100). Used as a metaphor for the soul. The poem has to do with the capturing and drawing-out of the soul from the innermost recesses of the self.

ATLAS. An atlas as a symbol of the world (p. 80); the mythical Atlas who upheld the heavens (p. 85); (used as a verb) to map out as for an atlas (p. 101).

CADAVER (p. 21 and elsewhere). The corpse immanent in all living flesh.

CHRIST-CROSS-ROW (p. 4). The crosses of a graveyard.

CRABS (p. 14). *Phthirius pubis.*

CRIB (p. 14). Brothel of the lower order.

CUPBOARD STONE (p. 65). The storehouse from which living flesh comes. The sense of the passage is roughly as follows: "Sir morrow" (the child of tomorrow, as yet unborn) will be waited upon by the "servant sun" which brings him to light and unfastens the cupboard of nature to furnish the naked egg of the seed with flesh, so that it may stand erect in the human form; the gristle will have a "gown" of bone; moisture as yet in the fog will turn the bones of death into living bone clothed with flesh.

ELOI (p. 36). A variation of Eli in *Eli, Eli, lama sabachthani,* "My God, my God, why hast thou forsaken me," the outcry of Jesus on the Cross. Hence, here a metaphor for the agony of those slain in battle.

EXODUS (p. 63). Not a reference to the biblical Book of Exodus but to the exodus itself, which is part of the story of the Garden of Eden in that the captivity and the exodus resulted from the Fall.

FOLLY (p. 58). A steeple or tower, set as a goal in a steeplechase. The poem combines elements of the steeplechase and the fox hunt.

FORK. Dividing or branching out (pp. 14, 27); the loins (p. 80). One of Thomas' favorite words in the early poems, and usually ambiguous; the exact meaning or meanings must be determined by inspection of the context.

GENTLEMAN. In the sonnets, the sun; time (p. 72).

GRAINS. Grains of earth (p. 112); grains of dust (p. 133); waves of the sea, compared to a blowing field of grain (p. 170).

HANGING ALBATROSS (p. 76). A symbol of guilt, after the albatross hung round the Ancient Mariner's neck.

HOLLOW HULK (p. 35). The womb. The sense of the passage is "Half of the fellow comes from the father as the father creates, in the hollow womb, the image of himself, an image which he himself drew from Adam and the life-giving sea."

HORNY MILK (p. 35). "Horny" is slang for "lustful"; the "milk" is the female secretion under sexual stimulation. The passage describes the act of sex.

HYLEG IMAGE (p. 93). (Astrol.) The hyleg is the point of life, the position of planets and signs, etc., as influencing the condition, constitution, and fortunes of parts of the body; the "image" is a chart of the hyleg positions as related to a particular body, or is a symbol of propitious positions.

MAN-IRON SIDLE (p. 40). The sidling walk of one handcuffed or otherwise bound to another in man-irons. Here used of the hero as so bound to his "ghost."

MAN MORROW (p. 65). The child as yet unborn, the man of "tomorrow" in the general sense.

MAN-WAGING (p. 49). *See* War-bearing.

MAN OF WINTER (p. 2). Opposite of "boy of summer," old man.

MASTED VENUS (p. 63). Probably the venus's-basin, or wild teasel; the "mast" being the stem.

MNETHA (p. 8). A character in Blake's *Tiriel.* The name is probably an anagram for Athena(m). Mnetha's daughter is Heva, but there is no real particularity in Thomas' allusion; he is merely saying that Jesus, as yet unconceived, was utterly formless, and had every and no relation to everything and everybody, as a consequence.

O (p. 21). Zero; symbol of nothing.

OIL. *See* Wax.

PARHELION (p. 36). A mock-sun; hence, "to bone of stars and blood of mock-suns."

PHOENIX (pp. 120–22). The mythical bird is here used as a symbol of heavenly aspiration. *See also* Saint.

RIDERLESS (pp. 42, 108). Undirected by the soul or ghost; thus, dead. The metaphor is that of the riderless horse.

ROOKING (p. 13). Thieving. The idea is that a girl might steal him and put him into her womb. The same notion occurs in "A Prospect of the Sea," *Selected Writings,* p. 109.

SAINT. The "saint carved and sensual," also called a "nun," is a "symbol of desire beyond my hours / And guilts, great crotch and giant / Continence," thus, of death. The phoenix (see above) and the saint seek to lure him to death, but his living beloved holds him to earth (pp. 120–22). The heron is called "saint" because viewed as the chaplain attending the execution of small birds by the hangman hawk (pp. 187–89).

SALT. Almost everywhere connected with the sea and the principle of life, or with the labor of Adam in the sweat of his brow. An exception is "the salt person"(p. 86), which is a reference to Lot's wife, who was turned into a pillar of salt.

SAMSON OF YOUR ZODIAC (p. 130). The enemy airman who will bomb London and bring down the heavens upon it as Samson overthrew the temple.

SARGASSO (p. 5). The tomb, which is to life as the Sargasso is to the sea. There is reference to the old notion that all lost ships drifted at last to the Sargasso; so the tomb takes all.

SCISSORS. A death-symbol (pp. 12, 21, 101); a birth-symbol. So too with "tailors" (p. 147); the "tailors" sew the suit of flesh, snipping it to fit, but also sew the shroud for it.

SEA. Almost invariably a life-symbol, if something emerges from it; a death-symbol if something goes back to it or "sails out" to it.

SEA-SUCKED ADAM (p. 35). The mortal body derived from Adam, drawn out of the sea. *See* Hollow hulk.

STAMMEL FEATHER (p. 37). A feather the shade of red used in stammel cloth (a coarse woolen fabric). The "feather" is of course "death's feather," a phrase very frequent in the early poems. The point here is that the "halves" have asked what the color of death is; they are answered that it is the color of the blood in the vein, since that very blood brings death, has death already immanent in it.

STRAW. Rays of light (p. 4). A metaphor for the frail prison of the girl's body, through which the speaker would break to be born (p. 13). Also associated with death, the "dry Sargasso of the tomb."

TAILOR. *See* Scissors.

TO-MORROW'S DIVER (p. 35). The unconceived child, thought of as "diving" into the future.

VENUSWISE (p. 52). Like Venus. The reference is to the mythical formation of the Milky Way through the expression of milk from Venus' breast.

WAR-BEARING (p. 49). A metathesis, like "man-waging," of a common phrase, to produce metaphor. The normal reading would be war-waging and man-bearing; by the exchange Thomas sets war as a metaphor for conception (the seed storming the womb). There is a similar exchange in "the man in the wind and the west moon" (p. 77).

WAX. A symbol of dead or mortal flesh, as opposed to oil, a life-symbol. See chap. vi, n. 21.

WEATHER. Almost invariably used for "season."

WHITE SEED (p. 133). Snow, considered as "sown."

WIDDERSHIN EARTH (p. 55). (Witchcraft) Variation of *withershins:* going in a direction contrary to the apparent motion of the sun; hence the earth has "widdershin" motion. Witches performed incantations by widdershin motion; the spell was undone if the motion was detected.

WOMB-EYED (p. 66). Seeing even in the womb; used here of the child foreknowing life, even in the womb.

X (p. 25). The cross put by the illiterate to serve as a signature; i.e., the tongue needs no words among the illiterate worms.

*Appendix C* BIBLIOGRAPHY

In compiling this list, foreign sources, including available periodicals, indexes, and anthologies, as well as the standard English-language reference sources have been examined in an effort to make this listing as complete as possible. The foreign sources have been checked through November, 1953, and the English through January, 1954. The phrase "Not verified" has been used after an entry which could not be adequately verified.

The Bibliography is in two parts, each arranged chronologically. Part I is comprised of books, poems, short stories, miscellaneous works, and radio broadcasts by Thomas. Part II contains critical, explicative, and biographical materials about Thomas and reviews of his works found in books, periodicals, and newspapers. Thomas' contributions to anthologies have been entered under the publication date of the anthology.

First lines, or identifying portions, have been placed in brackets following those poems which were published under only the title "Poem." Reviews and comments on individual books by Thomas may be found by referring to the entry number appearing after "Reviews" at the end of the citation for the particular book.

I wish to thank members of the staff of the British Broadcasting Corporation, particularly those in the External Broadcasting Division, for both their helpfulness and their generosity in responding to my request for information regarding Thomas' work with the B.B.C. In addition to a listing of his radio appearances, I received several unpublished typescripts of his broadcasts. These have been incorporated into the holdings of the Northwestern University Library and are indicated in this listing by an asterisk placed at the end of the entry.

Most of the material listed was available at the Northwestern University Library. However, the Modern Poetry Collection in the Harriet Monroe Room at the University of Chicago was very useful in locating many references. Assistance was also received from the libraries of Brown University, Harvard University, and Vassar College.

Several known omissions have occurred; among them are the following little magazines to which Thomas has contributed: *The Booster, Caravel,* and *Programme.* It is hoped it will be possible to include these later in a revision of this listing, for which I shall be glad to receive additions or corrections.

WILLIAM H. HUFF

# I. WORKS BY THOMAS

## 1933

### POEMS

1. "No Man Believes Who, When a Star Falls Shot," *Adelphi,* n.s., 6 (September, 1933), 398.

## 1934

### BOOKS

2. *18 Poems.* ("Sunday Referee Poets," Vol. II.) London: Sunday Referee and Parton Bookshop, 1934.

   *18 Poems.* London: Fortune Press, [1934]. Reissue.
   Reviews: 220, 221.

### POEMS

3. "The Woman Speaks" ["No food suffices but the food of death"], *Adelphi,* n.s., 7 (March, 1934), 399–400.

4. "Poem" ["Our eunuch dreams, all seedless in the light"], *New Verse,* No. 8 (April, 1934), 11–12.

5. "Two Poems" ["When once the twilight locks no longer"]; ["I see the boys of summer in their ruin"], *New Verse,* No. 9 (June, 1934), 6–9.

6. "Poem" ["If I were tickled by the rub of love"], *New Verse,* No. 10 (August, 1934), 8–9.

7. "Poem" ["From love's first fever to her plague . . ."], *The Criterion,* 14 (October, 1934), 27–28.

8. "Poem" ["Half of the fellow father as he doubles"], *New Verse,* No. 12 (December, 1934), 10–12.

9. "Poem in October," in DENYS K. ROBERTS *et al.* (eds.), *The Year's Poetry, 1935,* pp. 141–42. London: John Lane, Bodley Head, 1935.

10. "Especially When the October Wind"; "Light Breaks Where No Sun Shines," *The Listener,* [1934?]. (Not verified.) These two poems appeared in *The Listener* prior to publication in *18 Poems.*

11. "A Process in the Weather of the Heart"; "The Force That through the Green Fuse Drives the Flower"; "Where Once the Waters of Your Face," *Sunday Referee,* [1934?]. (Not verified.) The above three poems appeared in the *Sunday Referee* prior to publication in *18 Poems.*

### SHORT STORIES

12. "After the Fair," *New English Weekly,* March 15, 1934. "Enemies," *New Stories,* June–July, 1934.
13. "The Tree," *Adelphi,* n.s., 9 (December, 1934), 143–49.

### MISCELLANEOUS

14. [A review of] *The Solitary Way* by WILLIAM SOUTAR; *Squared Circle* by WILLIAM MONTGOMERIE; *Thirty Pieces* by SYDNEY SALT, *Adelphi,* n.s., 8 (September, 1934), 418–20.
15. "Answers to an Enquiry," *New Verse,* No. 11 (October, 1934), 8–9. Thomas answers six questions concerning his poetry.

## 1935

### POEMS

16. "A Poem in Three Parts" ["I, in my intricate image, stride on two levels"], *New Verse,* No. 16 (August–September, 1935), 2–5.
17. "Poems for a Poem," *Life and Letters Today,* 13 (December, 1935), 73–75.
18. "Three Poems" ["The hand that signed the paper felled a city"]; ["Should lanterns shine, the holy face"]; ["I have longed to move away"], *New Verse,* No. 18 (December, 1935), 15–17.

### SHORT STORIES

19. "The Visitor," *The Criterion,* 14 (January, 1935), 251–59.
20. "The Visitor," in EDWARD O'BRIEN (ed.), *Best British Short Stories of 1935,* pp. 193–200. Boston: Houghton Mifflin Co., 1935.

### MISCELLANEOUS

21. [A review of] *Songs from Prison* by M. K. GANDHI, *Adelphi,* n.s., 9 (January, 1935), 255–56.

22. [A review of] *Into the Light, and Other Poems* by LYLE DONAGHY; *The Noise of History* by JOHN LEHMAN; *A Mad Lady's Garland* by RUTH PITTER, *Adelphi,* n.s., 9 (February, 1935), 312–14.

23. [A review of] *The Poems of John Clare,* ed. Y. W. TIBBLE, *Adelphi,* n.s., 10 (June, 1935), 179–81.

24. [A review of] *A Comparison of Literature* by R. D. JAMESON, *Adelphi,* n.s., 11 (October, 1935), 58–59.

## 1936

### BOOKS

25. *Twenty-five Poems.* ("Dent's Contemporary Verse Series.") London: J. M. Dent & Sons, Ltd., 1936.
    *Twenty-five Poems.* London: J. M. Dent & Sons, Ltd., [1944]. Reprint.
    Reviews: 225, 226, 378.

### POEMS

26. "Poem" ["Find meat on bones that soon have none . . ."], *Purpose,* 8 (April–June, 1936), 102–3.

27. "Two Poems" ["This was the crucifixion on the mountain"]; ["Foster the light nor veil the manshaped moon"], *Contemporary Poetry and Prose,* No. 1 (May, 1936), 2.

28. "Two Poems toward a Poem" ["From the oracular archives and the parchment"]; ["Let the tale's sailor from a Christian voyage"], *Contemporary Poetry and Prose,* No. 3 (July, 1936), 53.

29. "Two Poems" ["Then was my neophyte . . ."]; ["Today, this insect, and the world I breathe . . ."], *Purpose,* 8 (October–December, 1936), 230–32.

30. "The Force That through the Green Fuse Drives the Flower"; "Light Breaks Where No Sun Shines," in MICHAEL ROBERTS (ed.), *The Faber Book of Modern Verse,* pp. 334–35. London: Faber & Faber, 1936.

31. "Poem" ["Then was my neophyte . . ."], *Transition,* No. 25 (fall, 1936), 20–21.

SHORT STORIES

32. "The Lemon," *Life and Letters Today,* 14 (spring, 1936), 129–32.

33. "The Burning Baby," *Contemporary Poetry and Prose,* No. 1 (May, 1936), 10–13.

34. "The Orchards," *The Criterion,* 15 (July, 1936), 614–22.

35. "Mouse and the Woman," *Transition,* No. 25 (fall, 1936), 43–58.

### 1937

POEMS

36. "We Lying by Seasand," *Poetry,* 49 (January, 1937), 183.

SHORT STORIES

37. "A Prospect of the Sea," *Life and Letters Today,* 16 (spring, 1937), 65–70.

38. "Holy Six," *Contemporary Poetry and Prose,* spring, 1937. (Not verified.)

39. "Prologue to an Adventure," *Wales,* No. 1 (summer, 1937), 1–6.

40. "The Map of Love," *Wales,* No. 3 (autumn, 1937), 116–23.

### 1938

POEMS

41. "Poem for Caitlin," *Delta,* April, 1938, pp. 6–7.

42. "In Memory of Ann Jones," *Life and Letters Today,* 18 (summer, 1938), 45.

43. "Four Poems" ["When all my five and country senses see"]; ["O make me a mask and a wall to shut from your spies"]; ["Not from this anger"]; ["Spire cranes"], *Poetry,* 52 (August, 1938), 247–49.

44. "Poem" ["How shall my animal . . ."], *The Criterion,* 18 (October, 1938), 29–30.

45. "Poem" ["O make me a mask and a wall to shut from your spies"], *Life and Letters Today,* 19 (September, 1938), 59–60.

46. "When All My Five and Country Senses See"; "O Make Me a Mask and a Wall To Shut from Your Spies," *Poetry*, 53 (November, 1938), 107–8. Reprint of two of the sequence, "Four Poems," on the occasion of the announcement that Thomas had won the Oscar Blumenthal Prize for Poetry for a group of poems published in *Poetry* during its twenty-sixth year.

47. "Birthday Poem," *Life and Letters Today*, 20 (December, 1938), 42.

48. "Two Poems," *Seven*, No. 3 (winter, 1938), 17.

49. "In Memory of Ann Jones"; "Poem" ["How shall my animal . . ."]; "Poem for Caitlin," in JAMES LAUGHLIN IV (ed.), *New Directions 1938*, pp. [267–72]. Norfolk, Conn.: New Directions, 1938.

### SHORT STORIES

50. "The Peaches," *Life and Letters Today*, 19 (October, 1938), 76–95.

51. "The Orchards," in JAMES LAUGHLIN IV (ed.), *New Directions 1938*, pp. [256–64]. Norfolk, Conn.: New Directions, 1938.

52. Prose work, *Seven*, No. 2 (autumn, 1938). (Not verified.)

53. "Prologue to an Adventure," *Delta*, Christmas, 1938, pp. 7–12. This prose piece is taken from a book in progress.

### MISCELLANEOUS

54. "In the Direction of the Beginning" (prose fragment of a work in progress), in JAMES LAUGHLIN IV (ed.), *New Directions 1938*, pp. [265–66]. Norfolk, Conn.: New Directions, 1938.

## 1939

### BOOKS

55. *World I Breathe*. Norfolk, Conn.: New Directions, [1939]. "Seven hundred copies."

    Reviews: 243, 249, 253, 256, 257, 260, 264, 357.

56. *Map of Love: Verse and Prose*. London: J. M. Dent & Sons, Ltd., [1939].

    Reviews: 231, 236, 241, 242, 254, 286.

**POEMS**

57. "Poem in the Ninth Month," *Poetry* (London), 1 (February, 1939), 26–27.

58. "Poem" ["If my head hurt a hair's foot"], *Poetry* (London), 1 (April, 1939), [23].

59. "Poem" ["If my head hurt a hair's foot . . ."], *Kenyon Review*, 1 (summer, 1939), 283–84.

60. "To Others than You"; "Paper and Sticks"; "When I Woke," *Seven*, No. 6 (autumn, 1939), 5–7.

61. "Poem: Unluckily for a Death," *Life and Letters Today*, 23 (October, 1939), 66–68.

62. "Poem" ["When all my five and country senses see"], in THOMAS MOULT (ed.), *The Best Poems of 1939*, p. 22. New York: Harcourt, Brace & Co., [1939].

63. "Her Tombstone Told When She Died," *Poetry*, 55 (November, 1939), 66.

64. "Poem" ["Her tombstone told when she died"]; "Poem in the Ninth Month"; "January 1939"; "Poem" ["If my head hurt a hair's foot . . ."], in JAMES LAUGHLIN IV (ed.), *New Directions 1939*, pp. 94–98. Norfolk, Conn.: New Directions, 1939.

**SHORT STORIES**

65. "Enemies," *Yellowjacket*, March, 1939.

66. "An Adventure from a Work in Progress," *Seven*, No. 4 (spring, 1939), 45-48.

67. "Old Garbo," *Life and Letters Today*, 22 (July, 1939), 66–80.

68. "Extraordinary Little Cough," *Life and Letters Today*, 22 (September, 1939), 415–25.

69. "The Fight," *Life and Letters Today*, 23 (December, 1939), 326–39.

70. "Patricia, Edith, and Arnold," *Seven*, No. 7 (Christmas, 1939), 4–11.

71. "The Burning Baby"; "The School for Witches," in JAMES LAUGHLIN IV (ed.), *New Directions 1939*, pp. 79–85, 86–93. Norfolk, Conn.: New Directions, 1939.

## 1940

### BOOKS

72. *Portrait of the Artist as a Young Dog.* London: J. M. Dent & Sons, Ltd., 1940.

    *Portrait of the Artist as a Young Dog.* Norfolk, Conn.: New Directions, 1940.

    *Portrait of the Artist as a Young Dog.* [London]: British Publishers' Guild, Ltd., 1948. Reprint.

    *Portrait de l'artiste en jeune chien* ["Portrait of the Artist as a Young Dog"]. Trans. by F. DUFAW-LABEYRIE. [Paris]: Éditions de Minuit, 1947.

    Reviews: 244, 245, 246, 248, 250, 252, 255, 258, 259, 266, 267, 324.

### POEMS

73. "Poem: Once below a Time." *Life and Letters Today,* 24 (March, 1940), 274–75.

74. "When I Woke the Town Spoke"; "To Others than You," *Furioso,* 1 (spring, 1940), 18–19.

75. "Poem: There Was a Saviour," *Horizon,* 1 (May, 1940), 318–19.

76. "Poem: Into Her Lying Down Head," *Life and Letters Today,* 27 (November, 1940), 124–26.

77. "Poem: To Others than You," *Living Age,* 359 (November, 1940), 285.

78. "Out of the Sighs . . . ," in PHYLLIS M. JONES (ed.), *Modern Verse, 1900–1940,* pp. 187–88. London: Oxford University Press, 1940.

### SHORT STORIES

79. "The Burning Baby," in DORIAN COOKE *et al.* (eds.), *New Apocalypse: An Anthology of Criticism, Poems and Stories.* London: Fortune Press, 1940. (Not verified.)

## 1941

### POEMS

80. "Deaths and Entrances," *Horizon,* 3 (January, 1941), 12–13.

81. "On a Wedding Anniversary," *Poetry* (London), 1 (January 15, 1941), 91.

82. "Love in the Asylum," *Poetry* (London), 1 (May–June, 1941), 186.

83. "Ballad of the Long-legged Bait," *Horizon,* 4 (July, 1941), 9–12.

84. "Among Those Killed in the Dawn Raid was a Man Aged a Hundred," *Life and Letters Today,* 30 (August, 1941), 116.

85. "Deaths and Entrances," *Decision,* 2 (September, 1941), 66.

86. "Hunchback in the Park"; "Marriage of a Virgin," *Life and Letters Today,* 31 (October, 1941), 41–43.

87. "Twenty-four Years Remind the Tears of My Eyes," in EARL DANIELS (ed.), *Art of Reading Poetry,* p. 419. New York: Farrar & Rinehart, 1941.

88. "After the Funeral [In Memory of Ann Jones]"; "And Death Shall Have No Dominion"; "I Have Longed To Move Away"; "The Hand That Signed the Paper Felled a City," in CECIL DAY-LEWIS and L. A. G. STRONG (eds.), *A New Anthology of Modern Verse, 1920–1940,* pp. 187–90. London: Methuen & Co., 1941.

89. "Light Breaks Where No Sun Shines"; "Ten Sonnets": ["Altarwise by owl-light in the half-way house"]; ["Death is all metaphors, shape in one history"]; ["First there was the lamb on knocking knees"]; ["What is the metre of the dictionary?"]; ["And from the windy west came two-gunned Gabriel"]; ["Cartoons of slashes on the tide-traced crater"]; ["Now stamp the Lord's Prayer on a grain of rice"]; ["This was the crucifixion on the mountain"]; ["From the oracular archives and the parchment"]; ["Let the tale's sailor from a Christian voyage"]; "Twenty-four years remind the tears of my eyes"; "Poem" ["Into her lying down head"], in OSCAR WILLIAMS (ed.), *New Poems, 1940,* pp. 214–24. New York: Yardstick Press, 1941.

90. "Light Breaks Where No Sun Shines"; "The Force That through the Green Fuse Drives the Flower," in RICHARD ALDINGTON (ed.), *Viking Book of Poetry of the English Speaking World,* pp. 1204–5. New York: Viking Press, 1941.

SHORT STORIES

91. "A Visit to Grandpa's," *Penguin New Writing*, 6 (May, 1941), 97–103. Reprinted from Thomas' *Portrait of the Artist as a Young Dog*.

92. "The Peaches," *Penguin New Writing*, 8 (July, 1941), 17–35. Originally a part of Thomas' *Portrait of the Artist as a Young Dog*.

93. "A Fine Beginning," in JOHN LEHMANN (ed.), *Folios of New Writing*, pp. 19–27. London: Hogarth Press, 1941.

94. "Extraordinary Little Cough," *Penguin New Writing*, 11 (November, 1941), 74–83.

## 1942

POEMS

95. "Ballad of the Long-legged Bait," *Partisan Review*, 9 (March–April, 1942), 137–50.

96. "Request to Zeda," *Horizon*, 6 (July, 1942), 6.

97. "The Force That through the Green Fuse Drives the Flower"; "Hand That Signed the Paper Felled a City"; "Light Breaks Where No Sun Shines"; "When All My Five and Country Senses See," in LOUIS UNTERMEYER (ed.), *Modern British Poetry*, pp. 495–96. 5th rev. ed. New York: Harcourt, Brace & Co., 1942.

98. "Ballad of the Long-legged Bait"; "And Death Shall Have No Dominion"; "Poem" ["There was a saviour"]; "The Marriage of a Virgin"; "The Hunchback in the Park," in OSCAR WILLIAMS (ed.), *New Poems, 1942*, pp. 227–41. Mount Vernon, N.Y.: Peter Pauper Press, 1942.

99. "Deaths and Entrances"; "On a Wedding Anniversary," in M. J. TAMBIMUTTU (ed.), *Poetry in War Time*, pp. 169–71. London: Faber & Faber, 1942.

## 1943

BOOKS

100. *New Poems*. ("Poets of the Year Series," 1943, No. 2.) Norfolk, Conn.: New Directions, 1943.
   Reviews: 274, 277, 278, 280, 281, 282, 284, 288.

POEMS

101. "Last Night I Dived My Beggar Arm"; "Poem" ["Your breath was shed"], *Poetry* (London), 2 (January–February, 1943), 34.

102. ["Poem"], *Wales,* No. 2 (October, 1943). (Not verified.)

103. "Deaths and Entrances"; "In Memory of Ann Jones," in OSCAR WILLIAMS (ed.), *New Poems 1943,* pp. 248–51. New York: Howell, Soskin & Co., 1943.

MISCELLANEOUS

104. *These Are the Men.* British Ministry of Information Films, 1943. A documentary war film containing "Special verse by Dylan Thomas superimposed upon Leni Riefenstahl's official Nazi film record of a pre-war Nuremberg festival, . . ."

105. "Our Country," *Wales,* No. 14 (October, November, December, 1943), 76–78. Commentary by Thomas for the first two reels of the five-reeler documentary film, *Our Country,* produced by John Eldridge and J. Jago of the Strand Film Company.

## 1944

POEMS

106. "Poem" ["On no work of words . . ."]; "Poem" ["Once it was the colour of saying"]; "Poem" ["We lying by sea-sand . . ."]; "Poem" ["The spire cranes"]; "In Memory of Ann Jones"; "Poem in October"; "Poem for Caitlin," in KEID-RYCH RHYS (ed.), *Modern Welsh Poetry,* pp. 120–27. London: Faber & Faber, 1944.

107. "Among Those Killed in the Dawn Raid Was a Man Aged a Hundred"; "To Others than You"; "When I Woke," in OSCAR WILLIAMS (ed.), *New Poems 1944,* pp. 159–61. New York: Howell, Soskin & Co., 1944.

108. "Among Those Killed in the Dawn Raid Was a Man Aged a Hundred"; "The Marriage of a Virgin," in ALLEN COMFORT and JOHN BAYLISS (eds.), *New Road, 1944: New Directions in European Art and Letters,* p. 170. London: Grey Walls Press, 1944.

## 1945

POEMS

109. "Vision and Prayer"; "Holy Spring," *Horizon*, 11 (January, 1945), 8–14.
110. "Poem in October," *Poetry*, 65 (February, 1945), 257–59.
111. "Poem in October," *Horizon*, 11 (February, 1945), 82–83.
112. "Holy Spring," *Sewanee Review*, 53 (April, 1945), 259.
113. "A Refusal To Mourn the Death, by Fire, of a Child in London," *New Republic*, 112 (May 14, 1945), 675.
114. "Lie Still, Sleep Becalmed," *Life and Letters Today*, 45 (June, 1945), 155.
115. "This Side of the Truth"; "Conversation of Prayers," *Life and Letters Today*, 45 (July, 1945), 28–29.
116. "Winter's Tale," *Poetry*, 66 (July, 1945), 175–80.
117. "This Side of the Truth," *New Republic*, 113 (July 2, 1945), 20.
118. "Conversation of Prayers," *New Republic*, 113 (July 16, 1945), 76.
119. "Vision and Prayer," *Sewanee Review*, 53 (July, 1945), 413–24.
120. "Fern Hill"; "A Refusal To Mourn the Death, by Fire, of a Child in London," *Horizon*, 12 (October, 1945), 221–23.
121. "In My Craft or Sullen Art," *Life and Letters Today*, 47 (October, 1945), 31.
122. "Ceremony after a Fire Raid," *Accent*, 5 (winter, 1945), 69–70.
123. "Fern Hill," *Nation*, 161 (December 15, 1945), 664.
124. "A Refusal To Mourn the Death, by Fire, of a Child in London," in RICHARD EBERHART and SELDEN RODMAN (eds.), *War and the Poet*, pp. 200–201. New York: Devin-Adair Co., 1945.
125. "The Hand That Signed the Paper Felled a City"; "Holy Spring"; "Ceremony after a Fire Raid"; "A Refusal To Mourn the Death, by Fire, of a Child in London," in OSCAR WILLIAMS (ed.), *The War Poets*, pp. 432–35. New York: John Day Co., 1945.

SHORT STORIES

126. "Reminiscences of Childhood," *The Listener,* 29 (February 25, 1943), 246–47. Autobiographical sketch incorporating the poem "Hunchback in the Park" and excerpts from Thomas' early poetry.

127. "Memories of Christmas," *The Listener,* 34 (December 20, 1945), 734–35.

### 1946

BOOKS

128. *Selected Writings.* ("New Directions Series of Selected Writings," No. 1.) New York: New Directions, 1946. Introduction to Thomas' poetry by JOHN L. SWEENEY.
Reviews: 297, 298, 299, 300, 302, 314, 324.

129. *Deaths and Entrances.* London: J. M. Dent & Sons, Ltd., 1946. *Deaths and Entrances.* London: J. M. Dent & Sons, Ltd., 1949. Reprint.
Reviews: 296, 307, 310, 315, 324, 378.

POEMS

130. "Conversation of Prayers," *New Republic,* 114 (April 29, 1946), 620.

131. "Fern Hill"; "The Force That through the Green Fuse Drives the Flower"; "A Refusal To Mourn the Death, by Fire, of a Child in London"; "The Marriage of a Virgin"; "Light Breaks Where No Sun Shines"; "Twenty-four Years"; "The Hunchback in the Park"; "The Hand That Signed the Paper Felled a City"; "And Death Shall Have No Dominion"; "Sonnets," in OSCAR WILLIAMS (ed.), *A Little Treasury of Modern Poetry,* pp. 75, 78, 222, 372, 379, 400, 423, 463, 478. New York: Charles Scribner's Sons, 1946.

132. "Poem" ["It is the sinner's dust-tongued bell claps me to churches . . ."], in WILLIAM PHILLIPS and PHILIP RAHV (eds.), *The Partisan Reader,* pp. 230. New York: Dial Press, 1946.

133. "Poem in October," in STEPHEN SPENDER, *Poetry since 1939,* pp. 45–47. New York: Longmans, Green & Co., 1946.

SHORT STORIES

134. "Quite Early One Morning," *Wales,* No. 23 (autumn, 1946), 83–86.

135. "Memories of Christmas," *Wales,* No. 24 (December, winter, 1946), 10–14. Read by Thomas, December 16, 1945, on a B.B.C. program and printed in *The Listener,* December 20, 1945.

MISCELLANEOUS

136. "How To Begin a Story," *The Listener,* 36 (October 17, 1946), 508. (Humorous essay.)

## 1947

POEMS

137. "In Country Sleep," *Atlantic Monthly,* 180 (December, 1947), 83–85.

138. "In Country Sleep," *Horizon,* 16 (December, 1947), 302–5.

139. "This Bread I Break"; "And Death Shall Have No Dominion"; "Poem in October"; "In My Craft or Sullen Art," in A. S. COLLINS (ed.), *Treasury of Modern Poetry,* pp. 206–10. London: University Tutorial Press, 1947.

140. "The Force That through the Green Fuse Drives the Flower," in RICHARD ALDINGTON (ed.), *Poetry of the English Speaking World,* p. 904. London: William Heinemann, Ltd., 1947.

141. "A Refusal To Mourn the Death, by Fire, of a Child in London"; "Vision and Prayer," in OSCAR WILLIAMS (ed.), *A Little Treasury of Great Poetry,* pp. 128, 238–44. New York: Charles Scribner's Sons, 1947.

SHORT STORIES

142. "Just like Little Dogs," *Wales,* [1947?]. (Not verified.) A reference to this story is made in *Wales,* No. 26 (summer, 1947) (p. 247), to its appearance in *"Wales* earlier issues."

MISCELLANEOUS

143. "The Crumbs of One Man's Year," *The Listener,* 36 (January 2, 1947), 28–29. (Prose sketch.)

144. "Holiday Memory," *Vogue,* July 15, 1947, p. 37. An auto-biographical sketch of Thomas' boyhood recollections of a holiday spent at the beach.

## 1948

### POEMS

145. "In My Craft or Sullen Art"; "Poem in October"; "To Others than You," in MAURICE WOLLMAN (ed.), *Poems of the War Years,* pp. 13, 60, 196. London: Macmillan Co., Ltd., 1948.

146. "Poem" ["Last night I dived my beggar arm"]; "Poem" ["Your breath was shed"], in JOHN ARLOTT (ed.), *First Time in America: A Selection of Poems Never Before Published in the U.S.A.,* pp. 181–82. New York: Duell, Sloane & Pearce, 1948.

147. "Poem in October"; "Fern Hill," *Merkur,* 2 (1948), 188–93. (Trans. by KURT HEINRICH HANSEN.) German translation of these poems with English on opposite pages.

148. "The Force That through the Green Fuse Drives the Flower," in *A Book of Modern Verse,* p. 62. London: Zodiac Books, 1948.

### MISCELLANEOUS

149. "Poem in October"; "In My Craft or Sullen Art," in LLOYD FRANKENBERG (ed.), *Pleasure Dome: A Collection of Phonograph Records of Various Poets Reading Their Own Works.* Columbia Records, Inc., n.p., 1948. Thomas reads from works chosen from his *Selected Poems.* (Set MM-877, 12″, 78 rpm.)

## 1949

### BOOKS

150. *Twenty-six Poems.* New York: New Directions, 1949. Printed in Italy. "The edition consists of ten copies . . . numbered I to X, and 140 copies . . . numbered 11 to 150. . . ." Copy examined is No. 112. Contains author's autograph.

### POEMS

151. "Over Sir John's Hill," *Botteghe oscure,* 4 (1949), 397–99; "Sopra al colle di Sir John" ["Over Sir John's Hill"], *Botteghe*

*oscure,* 4, supp. (December, 1949), 90–92. (Trans. by SAL-
VATORE ROSATI.)

152. "Digt i Oktober" ["Poem in October"], *Ord och Bild,* 58
(1949), 321–22. (Trans. by JØRGEN ANDERSEN.)

153. "Among Those Killed in the Dawn Raid Was a Man Aged a
Hundred"; "Poem in October"; "The Conversation of
Prayers"; "In My Craft or Sullen Art"; "Out of the Sighs
. . ."; "And Death Shall Have No Dominion"; "Ears in the
Turrets . . ."; "The Force That through the Green Fuse Drives
the Flower"; "I Dreamed My Genesis . . . ," in GEORGES-AL-
BERT ASTRE (ed.), *Anthologie de la poésie anglaise contem-
poraine,* pp. 186–211. Paris: L'Arche, 1949. Poems are in
English with French translation on opposite pages.

154. "A Grief Ago"; "When All My Five and Country Senses See";
"After the Funeral [In Memory of Ann Jones]," in ANNE
RIDLER (ed.), *A Little Book of Modern Verse,* pp. 150–53.
London: Faber & Faber, 1949.

155. "Poem" ["Especially when the October wind"]; "Poem"
["A process in the weather of the heart"]; "In Memory of Ann
Jones"; "And Death Shall Have No Dominion"; "In My Craft
or Sullen Art"; "Poem in October"; "Poem" ["The force that
through the green fuse drives the flower"]; "A Refusal To
Mourn the Death, by Fire, of a Child in London," in KENNETH
REXROTH (ed.), *The New British Poets,* pp. 241–50. Norfolk,
Conn.: New Directions, [1949].

156. "Light Breaks Where No Sun Shines," in STEFAN SCHIMANSKI
and HENRY TREECE (eds.), *A New Romantic Anthology,*
p. 180. London: Grey Walls Press, 1949.

157. "In My Craft or Sullen Art"; "And Death Shall Have No
Dominion," in SELDEN RODMAN (ed.), *100 Modern Poems,*
pp. 153, 191. New York: Pellegrini & Cudahy, 1949.

158. "The Force That through the Green Fuse Drives the Flower";
"The Hand That Signed the Paper Felled a City"; "Should
Lanterns Shine . . ."; "And Death Shall Have No Dominion";
"I Have Longed To Move Away," in GEOFFREY GRIGSON
(ed.), *Poetry of the Present,* pp. 208–11. London: Phoenix
House, 1949.

MISCELLANEOUS

159. "The Poet Answers a Critic," in *Dylan Thomas: "Dog among the Fairies."* London: Lindsay Drummond, Ltd., 1949. Pp. 149–50. Corrective comments by Thomas regarding explications of his poem "A Grief Ago" in the review by Miss Edith Sitwell of his *Twenty-five poems.*

## 1950

BOOKS

160. *Poems.* London: J. M. Dent & Sons, Ltd., 1950. Limited autographed edition.

POEMS

161. "Over Sir John's Hill," *Hudson Review,* 3 (autumn, 1950), 380–81.

162. "In the White Giant's Thigh," *Botteghe oscure,* 6 (November, 1950), 335–38. Sixty lines of a work in progress with an explanation by Thomas outlining "the plan of this long poem-to-be. . . ."

163. "Nella conscia del gigante bianco" ["In the White Giant's Thigh"], *Botteghe oscure,* 4, supp. (November, 1950), 20–23. (Trans. by SALVATORE ROSATI.)

164. "To Digte af Dylan Thomas: Poten naegter at begraede et barn omkommet ved en brand i London" ["A Refusal To Mourn the Death, by Fire, of a Child in London"]; "Bregne bakke" ["Fern Hill"], *Dialog,* 3 (1950), 171–73. (Trans. by Jørgen Nash.)

165. "Poem in October," in GEORGE WOODCOCK (ed.), *British Poetry Today,* pp. 1–15. ("Lecture Series," No. 7.) Vancouver, Canada: University of British Columbia, 1950.

166. "The Force That through the Green Fuse Drives the Flower"; "In Memory of Ann Jones"; "The Marriage of a Virgin," in DAVID DAICHES and WILLIAM CHARVAT (eds.), *Poems in English, 1530–1940,* pp. 634–36. New York: Ronald Press Co., 1950.

167. "The Force That through the Green Fuse Drives the Flower"; "And Death Shall Have No Dominion"; "A Refusal To Mourn

the Death, by Fire, of a Child in London"; "Poem in October,"
in HERMANN PESCHMANN (ed.), *The Voice of Poetry* (*1930–
1950*), pp. 191–96. London: Evans Bros., 1950.

168. "The Force That through the Green Fuse Drives the Flower";
"The Hand That Signed the Paper Felled a City"; "Death
Shall Have No Dominion," in CARLO IZZO (comp.), *Poesia
inglese contemporanea da Thomas Hardy agli Apocalittici*,
pp. 448–53. Modena, Italy: Guando, 1950. The above poems
appear in English with Italian translation on facing pages.

SHORT STORIES

169. "A Child's Memories of Christmas in Wales," *Harper's Bazaar*,
No. 2869 (December, 1950), 86–87+.

MISCELLANEOUS

170. "How To Be a Poet; or the Ascent of Parnassus Made Easy:
A Worldly Lecture in Two Parts by Dylan Thomas," *Circus*,
1 (April, 1950), 7–12; 1 (May, 1950), 5–8. This piece is illustrated by Ronald Searle. The initial paragraph in this essay
is not included in the reprint in *Atlantic Monthly* for July,
1951.

1951

POEMS

171. "In the White Giant's Thigh," *Atlantic Monthly*, 188 (September, 1951), 31–32.

172. "Do Not Go Gentle into That Good Night"; "Lament" ["When
I was a windy boy and a bit"], *Botteghe oscure*, 8 (November,
1951), 208–10.

173. "Poem on His Birthday," *World Review*, n.s., 32 (October,
1951), 66–67.

174. "A Refusal To Mourn the Death, by Fire, of a Child in Lon-
don"; "Fern Hill"; "Vision and Prayer"; "Ceremony after a
Fire Raid"; "Among Those Killed in the Dawn Raid Was a
Man Aged a Hundred"; "The Hand That Signed the Paper
Felled a City"; "In Memory of Ann Jones"; "The Force That
through the Green Fuse Drives the Flower," in KIMON FRIAR

and JOHN M. BRINNIN (eds.), *Modern Poetry, American and British,* pp. 371–84. New York: Appleton-Century-Crofts, 1951.

175. "The Force That through the Green Fuse Drives the Flower"; "The Hand That Signed the Paper Felled a City"; "Among Those Killed in the Dawn Raid Was a Man Aged a Hundred"; "A Refusal To Mourn the Death, by Fire, of a Child in London," in MARK VAN DOREN (ed.), *Introduction to Poetry,* pp. 527–30. New York: William Sloane Associates, 1951.

176. "A Refusal To Mourn the Death, by Fire, of a Child in London"; "Light Breaks Where No Sun Shines"; "The Force That through the Green Fuse Drives the Flower"; "I See the Boys of Summer in Their Ruin"; "On No Work of Words . . ."; "Not from This Anger"; "I, in My Intricate Image Stride on Two Levels"; "Poem in October"; "Fern Hill"; "Over Sir John's Hill"; "In Country Sleep"; "Especially When the October Wind"; "Winter's Tale"; "In the White Giant's Thigh," in OSCAR WILLIAMS (ed.), *A Little Treasury of British Poetry: The Chief Poets from 1500 to 1950,* pp. 815–42. New York: Charles Scribner's Sons, 1951. A note by Thomas concerning the poem, "In the White Giant's Thigh," says that it "is intended to be a part of a long poem, 'In country heaven,' which is in preparation, I mean by 'in preparation' that some of the long poem is written down on paper, some of it is a rough draft in the head, and the rest of it is radiantly unworded in ambitious conjecture." The note continues, outlining the plan and substance of this poem to be.

177. "Bregne bakke" ["Fern Hill"]; "Poeten naegter at begraede et barn omkommet ved brand i London" ["A Refusal To Mourn the Death, by Fire, of a Child in London"], in JØRGEN NASH, *Vredens Sange,* p. 911. Copenhagen, Denmark: Jarl Borgen, 1951.

MISCELLANEOUS

178. "How To Be a Poet," *Atlantic Monthly,* 188 (July, 1951), 46–49. (Satiric essay.)

## 1952

### BOOKS

179. *In Country Sleep*. New York: New Directions, [1952].

   *In Country Sleep*. New York: [New Directions], [1952]. "One of 100 special copies printed on Stoneridge paper and signed by the author."

   Reviews: 366, 367, 369, 370, 375, 376, 378, 379, 382, 383, 384, 385, 387, 392.

180. *Collected Poems, 1934–1952*. London: J. M. Dent & Sons, Ltd., 1952.

   *Collected Poems, 1934–1952*. Norfolk, Conn.: New Directions, 1952.

   *Collected Poems, 1934–1952*. London: J. M. Dent & Sons, Ltd., 1952. Limited autographed edition bound in leather.

   Reviews: 368, 372, 377, 390, 393, 394, 395, 405, 409, 414, 415, 418, 419, 422, 425, 428, 430, 432, 434, 436, 438, 440, 441, 442, 443, 446, 450.

### POEMS

181. "Do Not Go Gentle into That Good Night"; "Lament" ["When I was a windy boy and a bit"], *Partisan Review*, 19 (January–February, 1952), 7–9.

182. "Fern Hill," in CHARLOTTE I. LEE (ed.), *Oral Interpretation*, pp. 463–65. Boston: Houghton Mifflin Co., 1952.

183. "Poem on His Birthday," *Atlantic Monthly*, 189 (March, 1952), 62–64.

184. "Digt i Oktober" ["Poem in October"], *Dialog*, 5 (September, 1952), 6–7. (Trans. by JØRGEN NASH.)

185. "Poem in October," in NORMAN C. STAGBERG and WALLACE L. ANDERSON (eds.), *Poetry as Experience*, pp. 424–26. New York: American Book Co., 1952.

186. "Over Sir John's Hill," in CLIFFORD DYMENT *et al.* (eds.), *New Poems, 1952*, pp. 149–50. London: Michael Joseph, 1952.

187. "A Refusal To Mourn the Death, by Fire, of a Child in London"; "Hunchback in the Park"; "And Death Shall Have No

Dominion"; "The Force That through the Green Fuse Drives the Flower"; "Light Breaks Where No Sun Shines"; "Fern Hill"; "Twenty-four Years Remind the Tears of My Eyes"; "Sonnets I-X"; "The Marriage of a Virgin"; "The Hand That Signed the Paper Felled a City"; "Poem in October"; "Vision and Prayer"; "Over Sir John's Hill"; "In Country Sleep"; "In My Craft or Sullen Art," in OSCAR WILLIAMS (ed.), *A Little Treasury of Modern Poetry English and American,* pp. 515–42. Rev. ed. New York: Charles Scribner's Sons, 1952.

188. "A Refusal To Mourn the Death, by Fire, of a Child in London"; "Light Breaks Where No Sun Shines"; "In Memory of Ann Jones"; "Fern Hill"; "Poem in October," in OSCAR WILLIAMS (ed.), *Immortal Poems of the English Language,* pp. 612–15, 617. New York: Pocket Books, Inc., 1952.

189. ["Poems"], in NORMAN KREITMAN (ed.), *The Dove in Flames: An Anthology.* London: Housmans, 1952. (Not verified.) Contains two poems by Thomas; reference taken from *Poetry and Poverty,* No. 4 (1953).

### SHORT STORIES

190. "Visit to Grandpa's," in JOHN L. STEWART (ed.), *The Essay: A Critical Anthology,* pp. 473–79. New York: Prentice-Hall, Inc., 1952. Excerpt from *Portrait of the Artist as a Young Dog.*

### MISCELLANEOUS

191. "Fern Hill"; "A Child's Christmas in Wales"; "Do Not Go Gentle into That Good Night"; "In the White Giant's Thigh"; "Ballad of the Long-legged Bait"; Ceremony after a Fire Raid," in *Dylan Thomas,* a recording made February 22, 1952, of Thomas reading the above poems and short story. New York: Caedmon Publishers, 1952. (TC1002 A&B, 12″, 33⅓ rpm.)

192. "Llareggub, a Piece for Radio Perhaps," *Botteghe oscure,* 9 (1952), 134–55. The first half of a verse play which Thomas, in a letter appended at the end of the fragment, says he hopes to complete "very shortly."

193. "Adventures in the Skin Trade," in *New World Writing*, pp. 158–89. ("Mentor Selection," No. 2.) New York: New American Library of World Literature, Inc., 1952. This is the first section of a novel in progress.

## 1953

### BOOKS

194. *The Doctor and the Devils*. London: J. M. Dent & Sons, Ltd., 1953.

    *The Doctor and the Devils*. Norfolk, Conn.: New Directions, 1953. Adapted from the story by Donald Taylor and put into the form of a film scenario by Thomas.

    Reviews: 391, 396, 397, 398, 399, 401, 403, 426.

### POEMS

195. "Prologue," *Atlantic Monthly*, 191 (January, 1953), 46.
196. "Vision and Prayer" (excerpt); "Fern Hill" (excerpt), *Time*, 61 (April 6, 1953), 112.
197. "I Have Longed To Move Away"; "This Side of the Truth (for Llewelyn)," *New York Times Book Review*, November 22, 1953, p. 2.
198. "Do Not Go Gentle into That Good Night," *Encounter*, 1 (December, 1953), 4.
199. "The Force That through the Green Fuse Drives the Flower"; "It Was Sweet To Drown in the Readymade Handy Water" (excerpt from "Poem" in *Selected Writings*), in JACQUES MARITAIN, *Creative Intuition in Art and Poetry*, pp. 264, 296–97. ("Bollingen Series," Vol. XXXV, No. 1.) New York: Pantheon Books, 1953.

### SHORT STORIES

200. "Le Bébé ardent" ["The Burning Baby"], *Les Lettres nouvelles*, 1 (March, 1953), 31–37. (Trans. by JEAN LE TROILLEUX.)

### MISCELLANEOUS

201. "If I Were Tickled by the Rub of Love"; "Should Lanterns Shine"; "And Death Shall Have No Dominion"; "A Refusal

To Mourn the Death, by Fire, of a Child in London"; "Winter's Tale"; "There Was a Saviour"; "Poem on His Birthday"; "Lament," second volume of recordings by Thomas reading his own poems. New York: Caedmon Publishers, 1953. (No. 1018, 12", 33⅓ rpm.)

202. "A Story," *Harper's Bazaar*, 87 (December, 1953), 100. "It is all about a day's outing . . . when I was so high and much nicer."

203. "Four Lost Souls," in *New World Writing*, pp. 192–207. ("Mentor Selection," No. 3.) New York: New American Library of World Literature, Inc., 1953. This is the second chapter of a novel in progress, the first having appeared in *New World Writing*, No. 2.

### 1954

#### MISCELLANEOUS

204. "Under Milk Wood," *Mademoiselle*, 38 (February, 1954), 110–22. One of the three versions of this play; illustrated with photographs by Rollie McKenna of Thomas' town and the townspeople.

## RADIO TALKS AND OTHER BROADCASTS MADE OVER THE BRITISH BROADCASTING CORPORATION SYSTEM, 1943–51

### 1943

205. "Reminiscences of Childhood." Thomas delivered this autobiographical story on the Home Service series, broadcast February 25, 1943. Printed in *The Listener*, 29 (February 25, 1943), 246–47.

### 1945

206. "Memories of Christmas." A talk for the Welsh Home Service Children's Hour series, broadcast December 16, 1945. Printed in *The Listener*, 34 (December 20, 1945), 734–35.

### 1946

207. "Books and Writers" series. A discussion on poetry and poets between Dylan Thomas and James Stephens, with Gerald Bullett as chairman, broadcast June 18, 1946.

208. "How To Begin a Story." A talk for the Home Service series, broadcast October 8, 1946. Printed in *The Listener*, 36 (October 17, 1946), 508.

209. "What Has Happened to English Poetry?" A "Freedom Forum" discussion between Dylan Thomas and Edward Shanks, with Anthony MacDonald as chairman, broadcast October 16, 1946.

210. "Holiday Memory." A talk for the Third Programme on memories of a childhood holiday by the sea, broadcast October 25, 1946. Printed in *The Listener*, 36 (November 7, 1946), 634–35.

211. "Walter De la Mare as Prose Writer." A talk for the Third Programme's "Living Writers" series, broadcast November 30, 1946.

212. "The Crumbs of One Man's Year." Broadcast December 27, 1946. Printed in *The Listener*, 37 (January 2, 1947), 28–29.

### 1947

213. "The Peaches." A short story in "The Wednesday Story" series, broadcast January 8, 1947.

214. "Sir Philip Sidney." The first of a West of England Home Service series about great writers, "Literature in the West," broadcast January 24, 1947.*

### 1948

215. A talk with Arthur Calder-Marshall, editor of *Books and Authors,* about the dearth of comic books. Broadcast February 14, 1948.

216. Introductory talk for "The English Festival of Spoken Poetry" program, broadcast July 30, 1948. Printed in *The Listener,* 40 (August 5, 1948), 205.

## 1949

217. On the "Arts Magazine" program, July 29, 1949, Thomas read his own selection from the poetry of Edward Thomas and commented upon some of the poems chosen.*

218. A talk forming part of "Swansea and the Arts." In this program three writers, a composer, and a painter (all Swansea men) talked about their art and about Swansea. Broadcast October 6, 1949.*

## 1951

219. "The Festival Exhibition." A talk on the Welsh Home Service, broadcast June 19, 1951.*

## II. WORKS ABOUT THOMAS

### 1935

220. ANONYMOUS. *New Verse,* No. 13 (February, 1935), 21–22. (Review of *18 Poems.*)

221. HAPPENSTALL, RAYNER. *Adelphi,* n.s., 9 (February, 1935), 314–15. (Review of *18 Poems.*)

### 1936

222. ANONYMOUS. *Times (London) Literary Supplement,* September 19, 1936, p. 750. (Review of *Twenty-five Poems.*)

223. ANONYMOUS. ["Dylan Thomas"], *London Mercury,* February, 1936. (Not verified.)

224. SITWELL, EDITH. "Four New Poets [William Empson, Ronald Bottrall, Dylan Thomas, Archibald MacLeish]," *London Mercury,* 33 (February, 1936), 383–90.

225. SITWELL, EDITH. "The Achievement of Mr. Dylan Thomas," *Sunday Times,* 1936. (Not verified.) A review of Thomas' *Twenty-five Poems* reprinted as "Appendix I. A New Poet" in Henry Treece's *Dylan Thomas,* pp. 145–48.

### 1937

226. CULLIS, MICHAEL F. "Mr. Thomas and Mr. Auden," *Purpose,* 9 (April–June, 1937), 101–4. A review and commentary on *Twenty-five Poems* and Auden's *Look Stranger!*

## 1938

227. SNAITH, STANLEY. "Bubble Reputation," *Library Review*, No. 46 (summer, 1938), 255–60. Brief mention of Thomas along with numerous other poets.

228. TREECE, HENRY, "Dylan Thomas and the Surrealists," *Seven*, No. 3 (winter, 1938), 27–30.

## 1939

229. ANONYMOUS. *The Listener*, 22 (October 19, 1939), 780.

230. ANONYMOUS. *Times (London) Literary Supplement*, August 26, 1939, p. 499.

231. CONNOLLY, CYRIL. *New Statesman and Nation*, 18 (September 16, 1939), 404. (Review of *The Map of Love*.)

232. DYMENT, CLIFFORD. *Time and Tide*, 20 (October 7, 1939), 1308.

233. HAYS, H. R. "Surrealist Influence in Contemporary English and American Poetry," *Poetry*, 54 (July, 1939), 202–9.

234. JONES, GLYN. "Dylan Thomas," *Welsh Review*, 2 (October, 1939), 179.

235. MUIR, EDWIN. *The Present Age from 1914*. ("Introductions to Literature," Vol. V.) London: Cresset Press, 1939. A brief comment on Thomas' poetry (pp. 220–21).

236. MUIR, EDWIN. "New Poetry," *Purpose*, 11 (October–December, 1939), 241–43. (Review of *The Map of Love*.)

237. PORTEUS, HUGH GORDON. *New English Weekly*, 15 (September 7, 1939), 15.

238. POWELL, CHARLES. *Manchester Guardian*, September 8, 1939, p. 3. (Not verified.)

239. TAMBIMUTTU, M. J. "First Letter," *Poetry* (London), 1 (February, 1939), 1–4. Page 3 contains a note on Thomas.

240. TAMBIMUTTU, M. J. "Second Letter," *Poetry* (London), 1 (April, 1939), [2].

241. WILLIAMS, CHARLES. "Review of Books," *Life and Letters Today*, 23 (November, 1939), 237–39. (Review of *The Map of Love*.)

## 1940

242. ABERPENNAR, DAVIES. "The Map of Love," *Wales*, No. 11 (winter, 1939–40), 306–8. (Review of *The Map of Love*.)

243. AIKEN, CONRAD. "Rocking Alphabet," *Poetry*, 56 (June, 1940), 159–61. (Review of *The World I Breathe*.)

244. ANONYMOUS. *Times (London) Literary Supplement*, April 6, 1940, p. 173. (Review of *Portrait of the Artist as a Young Dog*.)

245. ANONYMOUS. *Nation*, 151 (November 23, 1940), 512. (Review of *Portrait of the Artist as a Young Dog*.)

246. ANONYMOUS. *New Yorker*, 16 (October 26, 1940), 86. (Review of *Portrait of the Artist as a Young Dog*.)

247. ARNOLD, LILIAN. *John O'London's Weekly*, 43 (April 19, 1940), 90.

248. BERESFORD, J. D. *Manchester Guardian*, April 5, 1940, p. 3. (Review of *Portrait of the Artist as a Young Dog*.)

249. BOGAN, LOUISE. *New Yorker*, 15 (January 27, 1940), 52. (Review of *The World I Breathe*.)

250. DAVIES, RHYS. *Life and Letters Today*, 24 (March, 1940), 336. (Review of *Portrait of the Artist as a Young Dog*.)

251. DREW, ELIZABETH, and SWEENEY, JOHN L. *Directions in Modern Poetry*, pp. 110–12 and spot references. New York: W. W. Norton & Co., 1940.

252. DUPEE, F. W. *New Republic*, 103 (December 30, 1940), 906. (Review of *Protrait of the Artist as a Young Dog*.)

253. F[ITTS], D[UDLEY]. *Saturday Review of Literature*, 22 (May 11, 1940), 20. (Review of *The World I Breathe*.)

254. GRIGSON, GEOFFREY. "New Poetry," *Horizon*, 1 (January, 1940), 57–61. A brief critical comment on Thomas' *Map of Love* in joint reviewing of seven other poets.

255. HOUSER, MARIANNE. "Sketches of Youth," *New York Times Book Review*, December 29, 1940, p. 4. (Review of *Portrait of the Artist as a Young Dog*.)

256. MILLS, CLARK. "Aspects of Surrealism," *Voices*, No. 101 (spring, 1940), 47–51. References to the surrealistic element in Thomas' poetry and prose relative to *The World I Breathe*.

129

257. QUINN, KERKER. *Books,* February 25, 1940, p. 14. (Review of *The World I Breathe.*)

258. RITCHEY, JOHN. *Christian Science Monitor,* November 23, 1940, p. 12. (Review of *Portrait of the Artist as a Young Dog.*)

259. ROSENFELD, PAUL. *Books,* November 17, 1940, p. 26. (Review of *Portrait of the Artist as a Young Dog.*)

260. ROSENFELD, PAUL. *Nation,* 150 (March 2, 1940), 399. (Review of *The World I Breathe.*)

261. SCARFE, FRANCIS. "The Poetry of Dylan Thomas," *Horizon,* 2 (November, 1940), 226–39.

262. SYMONS, JULIAN. "Obscurity and Dylan Thomas," *Kenyon Review,* 2 (winter, 1940), 61–71.

263. SWINNERTON, FRANK. *Observer* (London), April 7, 1940, p. 6.

264. THOMPSON, DUNSTAN. *New Republic,* 102 (April 1, 1940), 447. (Review of *The World I Breathe.*)

265. VERSCHOYLE, DEREK. "Mr. Dylan Thomas," *Spectator,* 164 (April 5, 1940), 496.

266. WEST, ANTHONY. *New Statesman and Nation,* 19 (April 20, 1940), 542. (Review of *Portrait of the Artist as a Young Dog.*)

## 1941

267. BYRNE, BARRY. *Commonweal,* 33 (January 10, 1941), 307. (Review of *Portrait of the Artist as a Young Dog.*)

268. GREGORY, HORACE. "American Poetry, 1930–40," *Decision,* 1 (January, 1941), 24–29. A brief mention of the appearance of Thomas in recently published little magazines.

269. TAMBIMUTTU, M. J. "Fourth Letter," *Poetry* (London), 1 (January 15, 1941), 90.

270. TREECE, HENRY. "Corkscrew or Footrule," *Poetry* (London), 1 (May–June, 1941), 196–99.

271. WANNING, ANDREWS. "Criticism and Principles: Poetry of the Quarter," *Southern Review,* 6 (spring, 1941), 806–9.

### 1942

272. KUNITZ, STANLEY J., and HAYCRAFT, HOWARD. *Twentieth Century Authors,* p. 1397. New York: H. W. Wilson Co., 1942. A biographical sketch.

273. SCARFE, FRANCIS. *Auden and After: The Liberation of Poetry, 1940–1941,* pp. 101–17. London: George Routledge & Sons, Ltd., 1942.

### 1943

274. ANONYMOUS. *Nation,* 157 (September 18, 1943), 332. (Review of *New Poems.*)

275. ANONYMOUS. "Romantics and Others," *Poetry Review,* May–June, 1943, pp. 179–82.

276. ANSTEY, EDGAR. "The Cinema," *Spectator,* 170 (April 9, 1943), 338. (Review of *These Are the Men,* a documentary film on which Thomas collaborated.)

277. AVISON, MARGARET. *Canadian Forum,* 23 (September, 1943), 143. (Review of *New Poems.*)

278. BENÉT, WILLIAM R. *Saturday Review of Literature,* 26 (October 16, 1943), 24. (Review of *New Poems.*)

279. DAICHES, DAVID. "Contemporary Poetry in Britain," *Poetry,* 62 (June, 1943), 150–64. Several pages are devoted to Thomas and his influence as an apocalyptic poet on contemporary poetry.

280. FITTS, DUDLEY. *Saturday Review of Literature,* 26 (August 28, 1943), 9. (Review of *New Poems.*)

281. GREGORY, HORACE. *New York Times Book Review,* July 25, 1943, p. 19. (Review of *New Poems.*)

282. RODITI, EDOUARD. *Poetry,* 63 (October, 1943), 48. (Review of *New Poems.*)

283. SILLEN, SAMUEL. "Mr. Sillen Comments," *New Masses,* 47 (September 14, 1943), 24–25. Brief quote from one of Thomas' sonnets to point out obscurantism extant in modern poetry.

### 1944

284. AIKEN, CONRAD. *New Republic,* 110 (January 3, 1944), 26. (Review of *New Poems.*)

285. BREWSTER, GHISELIN. "Use of a Mango," *Rocky Mountain Review,* 8 (spring, 1944), 12.

286. LUNDKVIST, ARTUR. "Engelsk lyrik under kriget" ("English Poetry during War"), *Bonniers litterära magasin,* 13 (November, 1944), 770–75. Comment on Thomas' poetry in reference to *Map of Love.*

287. STEARNS, MARSHALL W. "Unsex the Skeleton: Notes on the Poetry of Dylan Thomas," *Sewanee Review,* 52 (July, 1944), 424–40.

288. UNTERMEYER, LOUIS. "Eight Poets," *Yale Review,* 33 (winter, 1944), 351. (Review of *New Poems.*)

### 1945

289. ARMSTRONG, MARTIN. "The Spoken Word: Contrasts," *The Listener,* 34 (December 27, 1945), 776. Brief comment on Thomas' B.B.C. Christmas broadcast, "Memories of Christmas."

290. HOFFMAN, FREDERICK J. "Further Interpretations," *Freudianism and the Literary Mind,* pp. 277–308. Baton Rouge, La.: Louisiana State University Press, 1945.

291. HORAN, R. "In Defense of Dylan Thomas," *Kenyon Review,* 7 (spring, 1945), 304–10.

292. PORTER, BERN. *Henry Miller: A Chronology and Bibliography,* p. 33. Baltimore: Waverly Press, 1945. Reference to Thomas, among numerous others, as having been a recipient of correspondence from Henry Miller.

293. STEARNS, MARSHALL W. "Explication of Thomas' Poem, 'After the Funeral' ['In Memory of Ann Jones']," *The Explicator,* 3 (May, 1945), 52.

294. STEARNS, MARSHALL. "A Critic Interprets a Poem," in S. SCHEMANSKI and H. TREECE (eds.), *Transformation 3.* London: Lindsay Drummond, Ltd., [1945?]. An explication of Thomas' poem, "Light Breaks Where No Sun Shines"; reprinted in Henry Treece's *Dylan Thomas,* Appendix III, pp. 151–55.

295. SYMONS, JULIAN. "Of Crisis and Dismay: A Study of Writing in the Thirties," in B. RAJAN and ANDRES PEARSE (eds.), *Focus One,* pp. 90–111. London: Denis Dobson, 1945.

## 1946

296. ANONYMOUS. *Wind and the Rain,* 3 (autumn, 1946), 159–62. (Review of *Deaths and Entrances.*)

297. ANONYMOUS. *Weekly Book Review,* December 15, 1946, p. 20. (Review of *Selected Writings.*)

298. ANONYMOUS. *New Republic,* 115 (December 2, 1946), 742. (Review of *Selected Writings.*)

299. ANONYMOUS. *New Yorker,* 22 (December 21, 1946), 99. (Review of *Selected Writings.*)

300. ANONYMOUS. "Passionate Pilgrim," *Time,* 48 (December 2, 1946), 112. (Review of *Selected Writings.*)

301. BOTTERILL, D. "Among the Younger Poets," *Life and Letters,* 51 (November, 1946), 93–94.

302. BRINNIN, J. M. *New York Times Book Review,* December 8, 1946, p. 24. (Review of *Selected Writings.*)

303. DAY-LEWIS, CECIL. *The Poetic Image,* pp. 122–28, 133. New York: Oxford University Press, 1948. The Clark Lectures given at Cambridge in 1946, containing on p. 122 a statement by Thomas on his method of creating poetry.

304. HOFFMAN, FREDERICK J., *et al. The Little Magazine,* p. 219. Princeton, N.J.: Princeton University Press, 1946. Reference to Thomas along with an excerpt from "Among Those Killed in the Dawn Raid. . . ."

305. MARTIN, E. W. "English Writing in War Time," *Semaphore,* A (1946), 6–13. Brief reference to Thomas as "leader of the new Romantic movement."

306. MIZENER, ARTHUR. "Poets," *Nation,* 163 (August 10, 1946), 160.

307. POTTS, PAUL. "The Poetry of Dylan Thomas," *Poetry Quarterly,* 8 (spring, 1946), 29–31. (Review of *Deaths and Entrances.*)

308. RHYS, KEIDRYCH. "Contemporary Welsh Literature," in *British Annual of Literature, 1946,* pp. 17–22. London: British Authors' Press, Ltd., [1946].

309. SAVAGE, D. S. "Poetry of Dylan Thomas," *New Republic,* 114 (April 29, 1946), 619–22.

310. SPENDER, STEPHEN. "Poetry for Poetry's Sake and Poetry beyond Poetry," *Horizon*, 13 (April, 1946), 221–38. Pages 233–35 contain criticism based on *Deaths and Entrances* with excerpts from Thomas' poems.

311. SPENDER, STEPHEN. *Poetry since 1939*. New York: Longmans, Green & Co., 1946. Chapter xii discusses Dylan Thomas, George Barker, and David Gascoyne.

312. STEPHENS, PETER J. "Dylan Thomas: Giant among Moderns," *New Quarterly of Poetry*, 1 (winter, 1946–47), 7–11.

313. TREECE, HENRY. "Gerard Manley Hopkins and Dylan Thomas," in *How I See Apocalypse*, pp. 129–39. London: Lindsay Drummond, Ltd., 1946.

### 1947

314. ANONYMOUS. *Booklist*, 43 (February 1, 1947), 166. (Review of *Selected Writings*.)

315. ANONYMOUS. *English Studies*, 28 (June, 1947), 91–92. (Review of *Deaths and Entrances*.)

316. FIEDLER, L. "The Latest Dylan Thomas," *Western Review*, 11 (winter, 1947), 103–6.

317. GIBSON, HENRY, "A Comment," *The Critic*, 1 (autumn, 1947), 20.

318. GREGORY, HORACE. "Romantic Heritage in the Writings of Dylan Thomas," *Poetry*, 69 (March, 1947), 326–36.

319. HECHT, ROGER. "Light and Darkness," *Bard Review*, 2 (spring, 1947), 57–58. Review of Thomas' writing as represented by the works chosen for *Selected Writings of Dylan Thomas*.

320. SITWELL, EDITH. "Comment on Dylan Thomas," *The Critic*, 1 (autumn, 1947), 18.

321. TINDALL, WILLIAM Y. *Forces in Modern British Literature, 1885–1946*, pp. 351–55. New York: A. A. Knopf, 1947. Contains numerous references of varied length to Thomas' poetry and prose and his influence on modern literature.

322. WILLIAMS, MICHAEL. "Welsh Voices in the Short Story," *Welsh Review*, 6 (winter, 1947), 290–98.

## 1948

323. ARNHEIM, RUDOLF, *et al. Poets at Work,* pp. 53–54, 60, 164. New York: Harcourt, Brace & Co., 1948. Brief notes on Thomas' poetry with a facsimile of a work sheet for the "Ballad of the Long-legged Bait."

324. ASTRE, GEORGES-ALBERT. "Un jeune et grand poète anglais," *Critique,* 4 (January, 1948), 21–29. French-language review and criticism of Thomas' poetry as represented by *Deaths and Entrances, Selected Writings,* and *Portrait of the Artist as a Young Dog.*

325. GRIGSON, GEOFFREY. *Harp of Aeolus and Other Essays on Art, Literature and Nature,* pp. 151–60. London: George Routledge & Sons, Ltd., 1948. Critical commentary on Thomas' poetry, finding it unfavorable in terms of "ineptitude," "faltering," and "awkwardness."

326. HUDDLESTONE, LINDEN. "An Approach to Dylan Thomas," *Penguin New Writing,* 35 (1948), 123–60.

327. KORG, JACOB. "The Short Stories of Dylan Thomas," *Perspective,* 1 (spring, 1948), 184–91.

328. LEWIS, E. GLYN. "Dylan Thomas," *Welsh Review,* 7 (1948), 270–81. An appreciation of Thomas' poetry.

329. MOORE, NICHOLAS. "The Poetry of Dylan Thomas," *Poetry Quarterly,* 10 (winter, 1948–49), 229–36.

330. RHYS, ANEURIN. "Dylan Thomas: A Further Estimate," *Poetry Review,* 39 (April–May, 1948), 214–16.

331. TINDALL, WILLIAM Y. "Poetry of Dylan Thomas," *American Scholar,* 17 (autumn, 1948), 431–39.

## 1949

332. ANONYMOUS. *British Annual of Literature, 1949,* p. 89. London: British Authors' Press, Ltd., [1949].

333. ASTRE, GEORGES-ALBERT. *Anthologie de la poésie anglaise contemporaine.* Paris: L'Arche, 1949. Pages 27–38 contain "La Réaction surréaliste et l'intériorisation Dylan Thomas."

334. BULLOUGH, GEOFFREY. *The Trend of Modern Poetry,* pp. 217–21. London: Oliver & Boyd, 1949. Criticism and commentary

on Thomas' poetry in a chapter entitled "Surrealism, the New Apocalypse."

335. Cox, R. G. "The Cult of Dylan Thomas," *Scrutiny*, 16 (September, 1949), 247–50. (Review of Henry Treece's book, *Dylan Thomas.*)

336. FRANKENBERG, LLOYD. *Pleasure Dome: On Reading Modern Poetry*. Boston: Houghton Mifflin Co., 1949. Pp. 316–23.

337. JONES, NOEL A. "Dylan Thomas as a Pattern," *British Annual of Literature, 1949*, pp. 12–16. London: British Authors' Press, Ltd., [1949].

338. KAPLAN, MILTON A. *Radio and Poetry*, p. 139. New York: Columbia University Press, 1949. A note referring to Thomas' use of assonance, internal and "slant" rhymes, to enrich the tonal quality of his verse.

339. REXROTH, KENNETH. *The New British Poets*. Norfolk, Conn.: New Directions, [1949]. Rexroth, in his Introduction (pp. vii–xxxviii), devotes several pages to criticisms of Thomas' work and influence as a poet.

340. RHYS, ANEURIN. "Dylan Thomas," *Poetry Quarterly*, 11 (summer, 1949), 119–20. (Review of Henry Treece's *Dylan Thomas.*)

341. RODMAN, SELDEN. *100 Modern Poems*. New York: Pellegrini & Cudahy, 1949. Pages xxviii–xxx contain notes on the work of Thomas.

342. TREECE, HENRY. *Dylan Thomas: "Dog among the Fairies."* London: Lindsay Drummond, Ltd., [1949]. 159 pp. A critical assessment of Thomas' work and factors influencing him, including comments by Thomas, several explications of poems, and a glossary of compound words and proper names in his early poems.

### 1950

343. ANDERSEN, KARL O. "Dylan Thomas," *Dialog*, 3 (1950), 174. A brief Danish-language consideration of Thomas and his work.

344. ANONYMOUS. "Dylan Thomas in Vancouver," *Contemporary Verse*, No. 31 (spring, 1950), 26–27.

345. AIVAZ, DAVID. "The Poetry of Dylan Thomas," *Hudson Review*, 3 (autumn, 1950), 382–404.

346. BREIT, H. "Talk with Dylan Thomas," *New York Times Book Review*, May 14, 1950, p. 19.

347. DAICHES, DAVID, and CHARVAT, WILLIAM (eds.). *Poems in English, 1530–1940*, pp. 744–45. New York: Ronald Press Co., 1950. Contains explicative notes on "The Force That through the Green Fuse Drives the Flower"; "In Memory of Ann Jones"; "The Marriage of a Virgin."

348. GIOVANNINI, G. "Thomas' 'The force that through the green fuse,'" *Explicator*, 8 (June, 1950), 59.

349. HYNES, SAM. "Thomas' 'From love's first fever to her plague,'" *Explicator*, 9 (December, 1950), 18.

350. IZZO, CARLO. "Dylan Thomas," *Poesia inglese contemporanea da Thomas Hardy agli Apocalittici*, pp. 543–44. Modena, Italy: Guando, [1950]. A critical biographical sketch of Thomas in Italian.

351. JOHNSON, S. F. "Thomas' 'The force that through the green fuse,'" *Explicator*, 8 (June, 1950), 60.

352. STALLMAN, ROBERT W. *The Critic's Notebook*, p. 64. Minneapolis: University of Minnesota Press, 1950. A reprint of a part of the statement in which Thomas comments on his own poetry in a letter to Henry Treece. *See* M. W. Stearns's "Unsex the Skeleton," *Sewanee Review*, summer, 1944. (No. 287.)

353. STEPHENS, PETER J. "Dylan Thomas: Giant among Moderns," *Poetry Book Magazine*, 2 (1950), 16. This essay appeared earlier in the *New Quarterly of Poetry*, winter, 1946–47. (*See* No. 312.)

354. WERRY, RICHARD R. "Poetry of Dylan Thomas," *College English*, 11 (February, 1950), 250–56.

355. WOODCOCK, GEORGE. *British Poetry Today*, pp. 1–15. ("Lecture Series," No. 7.) Vancouver, Canada: University of British Columbia, 1950. An address which includes comments on Thomas and his poetry, citing various lines as well as the whole of "Poem in October."

## 1951

356. ANONYMOUS. "In the White Giant's Thigh," *Atlantic Monthly,* 188 (November, 1951), 22–23. A discussion of the poem, "In the White Giant's Thigh."

357. BERRYMAN, JOHN. "The Loud Hill of Wales," in JOHN C. RANSOM (ed.), *The Kenyon Critics,* pp. 255–59. New York: World Publishing Co., 1951. An intensive review of Thomas' work based on *The World I Breathe,* reprinted from *Kenyon Review,* autumn, 1940.

358. BRINNIN, JOHN M. "Dylan Thomas in America," *Vassar Alumnae Magazine,* 37 (December, 1951), 12–15.

359. DEUTSCH, BABETTE. "Orient Wheat," *Virginia Quarterly Review,* 27 (April, 1951), 221–36.

360. FRIAR, KIMON, and BRINNIN, JOHN M. (eds.), *Modern Poetry: American and British,* pp. 540–41. New York: Appleton-Century-Crofts, 1951. Explication of "Vision and Prayer" and "In Memory of Ann Jones."

361. HUGHES, RICHARD. "Wales through the Looking-Glass," *The Listener,* 45 (May 24, 1951), 838–39. Favorable commentary on Thomas' writing and his position as an artist; a survey of Wales as portrayed by its artists with reference to the lack of general appreciation paid the artist by the public.

362. MILES, JOSEPHINE. *The Primary Language of Poetry in the 1940's,* pp. 383–542. ("University of California Publications in English," Vol. XIX, No. 3.) Berkeley and Los Angeles: University of California Press, 1951. A comparison and study of Thomas' poetic language is made throughout this work in conjunction with other poets of the period.

363. SCOTT-JAMES, R. A. *Fifty Years of English Literature.* London: Longmans, Green & Co., 1951. Brief references to Thomas and his place among the modern poets.

364. SEWELL, ELIZABETH. *The Structure of Poetry,* p. 128. London: Routledge & Kegan Paul, Ltd., 1951. Brief comparison of Thomas' poetry with the poetry of Rimbaud.

365. SVERDRUP, HAROLD. "Møte med Dylan Thomas" ["Meeting with Dylan Thomas"], *Vinduet,* 5 (summer, 1951), 476–80.

## 1952

366. ANONYMOUS. *Booklist,* 48 (May 15, 1952), 293. (Review of *In Country Sleep.*)

367. ANONYMOUS. *Chicago Sunday Tribune Magazine of Books,* April 13, 1952, p. 5. (Review of *In Country Sleep.*)

368. ANONYMOUS. "Salute to a Poet," *Times (London) Literary Supplement,* November 28, 1952, p. 776. (Review of *Collected Poems.*) A favorable, detailed, and comprehensive examination of Thomas' poetry.

369. BOGAN, LOUISE. "Books," *New Yorker,* 28 (August 2, 1952), 65. (Review of *In Country Sleep.*)

370. DEUTSCH, BABETTE. *New York Herald Tribune Book Review,* March 23, 1952, p. 4. (Review of *In Country Sleep.*)

371. DEUTSCH, BABETTE. "Alchemists of the Word," in *Poetry in Our Time,* pp. 312–47. New York: Henry Holt & Co., 1952.

372. DUCHENE, L. F. *Manchester Guardian,* November 14, 1952, p. 4. (Review of *Collected Poems.*)

373. DURRELL, LAWRENCE. "Poetry in the Thirties," in *Key to Modern Poetry,* pp. 196–208. London: Peter Nevill, Ltd., 1952. Contains brief references to Thomas.

374. EDMAN, IRWIN. "The Spoken Word," *Saturday Review,* 35 (November 29, 1952), 68–69. Mentions Thomas' manner and quality in poetry-reading.

375. FERLING, LAWRENCE. *San Francisco Chronicle,* March 9, 1952, p. 23. (Review of *In Country Sleep.*)

376. FRANKENBERG, LLOYD. "Controlled Abandon," *New York Times Book Review,* April 6, 1952, p. 4. (Review of *In Country Sleep.*)

377. FRASER, G. S. *New Statesman and Nation,* 44 (November 29, 1952), 640. (Review of *Collected Poems.*)

378. GREENHUT, MORRIS. "Opinion," *Beloit Poetry Journal,* 2 (summer, 1952), 28–29. A brief critical review of Thomas' *In Country Sleep,* poetry which "despite moving passages will do little to the reputation of the fine poet of *Twenty-five Poems* and *Deaths and Entrances.*"

379. HUMPHRIES, ROLFE. *Nation,* 174 (April 19, 1952), 389. (Review of *In Country Sleep.*)

380. JOHNSON, S. F. "Thomas' 'The Hunchback in the Park' and 'The Marriage of a Virgin,'" *Explicator,* 10 (February, 1952), 27.

381. JOHNSON, S. F. "Thomas' 'The force that through the green fuse . . . ,'" *Explicator,* 10 (February, 1952), 26.

382. McDONALD, G. D. *Library Journal,* 77 (March 15, 1952), 533. (Review of *In Country Sleep.*)

383. MEYER, G. P. "Bibliographical Sketch," *Saturday Review,* 35 (June 21, 1952), 17. (Review of *In Country Sleep.*)

384. ROSENBERG, JAMES L. *Talisman,* No. 2 (winter, 1952), 51–52. (Review of *In Country Sleep.*)

385. ROTHBERG, WINTERSET. *Poetry,* 81 (December, 1952), 184. (Review of *In Country Sleep.*)

386. SPENDER, STEPHEN. *Spectator,* 189 (December 5, 1952), 780.

387. SWEENEY, JOHN L. "Intimations of Mortality," *New Republic,* 126 (March 17, 1952), 18. (Review of *In Country Sleep.*)

388. TATE, ALLEN. "The Angelic Imagination: Poe and the Power of Words," *Kenyon Review,* 14 (summer, 1952), 460.

389. WILDER, AMOS N. *Modern Poetry and the Christian Tradition,* pp. 100–102. New York: Charles Scribner's Sons, 1952. Section entitled "Man and Nature in Dylan Thomas."

## 1953

390. ADAMS, PHOEBE. "Symbols and Metaphors," *Atlantic Monthly,* 191 (May, 1953), 79–80. (Review of *Collected Poems.*)

391. AGEE, JAMES. "A Dylan Thomas Screen Play," *New York Times Book Review,* December 6, 1953, p. 38. (Review of *The Doctor and the Devils.*)

392. ANONYMOUS. *Bookmark,* 12 (January, 1953), 81. (Review of *In Country Sleep.*)

393. ANONYMOUS. *Kirkus,* 21 (March 1, 1953), 169. (Review of *Collected Poems.*)

394. ANONYMOUS. "Welsh Rare One," *Time,* 61 (April 6, 1953), 112. (Review of *Collected Poems.*)

395. ANONYMOUS. *Booklist,* 49 (May 15, 1953), 299. (Review of *Collected Poems.*)

396. ANONYMOUS. "Film-script," *Times (London) Literary Supplement,* May 29, 1953, p. 351. (Review of *The Doctor and the Devils.*)

397. ANONYMOUS. *Manchester Guardian,* June 16, 1953, p. 4. (Review of *The Doctor and the Devils.*)

398. ANONYMOUS. *New Statesman and Nation,* 45 (June 27, 1953), 786. (Review of *The Doctor and the Devils.*)

399. ANONYMOUS. "A Lesson in Anatomy," *Time,* 62 (October 5, 1953), 110. (Review of *The Doctor and the Devils.*)

400. ANONYMOUS. "Mr. Dylan Thomas: Innovation and Tradition," *Times* (London), November 10, 1953, p. 11. An extraordinarily lengthy obituary paying high tribute to Thomas and summarizing his work briefly but informatively, mentioning his planned "work with Stravinsky on the *libretto* of an opera."

401. ANONYMOUS. *Booklist,* 50 (November 15, 1953), 116. (Review of *The Doctor and the Devils.*)

402. ANONYMOUS. "Obituary," *Time,* 62 (November 16, 1953), 93.

403. ANONYMOUS. "The Script of a Screenplay," *New York Herald Tribune Book Review,* November 29, 1953, p. 16. (Review of *The Doctor and the Devils.*)

404. ANONYMOUS. "Editorial Note: The Second Phase of New-Romanticism," *Poetry and Poverty,* No. 4 (1953), 4–5.

405. ANONYMOUS. "Poetry and Protest," *Poetry and Poverty,* No. 4 (1953), 39–40. (Review of *Collected Poems.*)

406. ANONYMOUS. *Encounter,* 1 (December, 1953), 3. A brief note on Thomas' death and telling of a forthcoming number of *Encounter* which will contain memoirs and appreciations of Dylan Thomas.

407. ANONYMOUS. "Obituary—Dylan Thomas," *Dock Leaves,* winter, 1953, pp. 4–7, 16. Page 16 contains a note regarding a Dylan Thomas Award to be given for the best poem in tribute to the memory of Thomas.

408. AUDEN, WYSTAN H., *et al.* "Dylan Thomas Fund," *Saturday Review*, 36 (December 5, 1953), 30.

409. BOWDEN, R. H. *Poetry Quarterly*, 14 (winter, 1952–53), 126–28. (Review of *Collected Poems.*)

410. BREIT, HARVEY. "Farewell and Hail," *New York Times Book Review*, November 22, 1953, p. 8. A brief memorial written regarding Thomas' death.

411. BROOKS, VAN WYCK. *The Writer in America*, p. 14. New York: E. P. Dutton & Co., 1953. A brief quote from a question asked by Thomas during a visit to America concerning the number of poets that teach in this country.

412. CAMPBELL, ROY. *Lorca: An Appreciation of His Poetry.* New Haven, Conn.: Yale University Press, 1953. Campbell makes a brief comparison of Lorca and Thomas in their use of euphonious words.

413. CLANCY, J. P. "Dylan Thomas: Promise Clipped," *America*, 90 (December 12, 1953), 295–96.

414. COFFMAN, STANLEY K., JR. *Books Abroad*, 27 (autumn, 1953), 436. (Review of *Collected Poems.*)

415. CORMAN, CID. "Dylan Thomas: Rhetorician in Mid-Career," *Accent*, 13 (winter, 1953), 56–59. (Review of *Collected Poems.*)

416. DAVENPORT, JOHN. "Dylan Thomas," *Twentieth Century*, 153 (February, 1953), 142–46.

417. DOBRÉE, BONAMY. "Two Experiments," *Spectator*, 190 (June 12, 1953), 763–64.

418. ENGLE, PAUL. "An Authentic Voice of Mid-Century: Dylan Thomas' Exciting, Baffling Poetry," *Chicago Sunday Tribune Magazine of Books*, April 5, 1953, p. 4. (Review of *Collected Poems.*)

419. FERLING, LAWRENCE. *San Francisco Chronicle*, April 12, 1953, p. 9. (Review of *Collected Poems.*)

420. FRASER, G. S. *The Modern Writer and His World.* London: Derek Verschoyle, Ltd., 1953. Scattered references to Thomas regarding his relation to movements in modern literature, primarily poetry.

421. FREMANTIC, ANNE. "Death of a Poet," *Commonweal,* 59
(December 18, 1953), 285–86. A lengthy obituary contain-
ing a short poem by John Logan entitled "Lines for the
Death of Dylan Thomas (November 9, 1953)."

422. GRADDON, JOHN. "The Interior Life," *Poetry Review,* 44
(April–June, 1953), 338–40. (Review of *Collected Poems.*)

423. HAYWARD, JOHN. "Dylan Thomas," *Bonniers litterära magasin,*
22 (October, 1953), 604–7. Swedish-language note on
Thomas entitled "Brev från London," translated from
English.

424. HEWES, HENRY. "Broadway Postscript: The Backward Town
of Llareggub," *Saturday Review,* 36 (June 6, 1953), 24–25.
Criticism of Thomas' play, *Under Milk Wood,* read by Thomas
with the assistance of five actors. It is a play which "seems
doomed to remain a reading piece."

425. JOHNSON, GEOFFREY. "The Acid Test," *Poetry Review,* 44
(April–June, 1953), 340–43. (Review of *Collected Poems.*)

426. JOOST, NICHOLAS. "The Problem of Loving and Hating," *Commonweal,* 59 (November 6, 1953), 126–27. (Review of *The
Doctor and the Devils.*)

427. LONGAKER, MARK, and BOLLES, EDWIN C. (eds.), "Dylan
Thomas," in *Contemporary English Literature,* pp. 294–96.
New York: Appleton-Century-Crofts, Inc., 1953.

428. MACNEICE, LOUIS. "The Strange, Mighty Impact of Dylan
Thomas' Poetry," *New York Times Book Review,* April 5,
1953, p. 1+. (Review of *Collected Poems.*)

429. MARITAIN, JACQUES. *Creative Intuition in Art and Poetry,*
pp. 74, 194 n. ("Bollingen Series," Vol. XXXV, No. 1.) New
York: Pantheon Books, 1953.

430. MAYHEAD, ROBIN. "Dylan Thomas," *Scrutiny,* 19 (winter,
1952), 142–47. (Review of *Collected Poems.*) "Mr. Thomas'
art has not improved with the years. . . . Superior as they
are, generally speaking, to the later productions, the early
poems could hardly have given one much hope for the
future."

431. "Modernism in Poetry Yes and No; Readers' Free-for-All,"

*Poetry Review*, 44 (October–December, 1953), 454–56. A series of comments by readers concerning Thomas' poetry and the reviews by John Graddon and Geoffrey Johnson in the April–June, 1953, issue of *Poetry Review*.

432. MUIR, EDWIN. *Britain Today*, [1953?]. (Review of *Collected Poems*.) Reference taken from inside back cover of *Poetry and Poverty*, No. 4. (Not verified.)

433. READ, HERBERT. *The True Voice of Feeling*, p. 86. London: Faber & Faber, 1953.

434. RIGGS, THOMAS, JR. "Recent Poetry—a Miscellany," *Nation*, 176 (May 2, 1953), 376–78. (Review of *Collected Poems*.)

435. ROLO, CHARLES J. "Reader's Choice," *Atlantic Monthly*, 192 (November, 1953), 110.

436. SCOTT, W. T. "Wild Man Bound," *Saturday Review*, 36 (April 11, 1953), 29–30. (Review of *Collected Poems*.)

437. SHUTTLEWORTH, MARTIN. "Without Apologies," *New Statesman and Nation*, 40 (February 7, 1953), 144–45. A stinging observation of a particular "literary" luncheon held in honor of Thomas' receipt of the Foyle Award.

438. SITWELL, EDITH. "The Love of Man, the Praise of God," *New York Herald Tribune Book Review*, May 10, 1953, p. 1+. (Review of *Collected Poems*.)

439. SPENDER, STEPHEN. "Movements and Influences in English Literature, 1927–1952," *Books Abroad*, 27 (winter, 1953), 5–32. On page 29 there is a consideration of Thomas' influence during the latter part of the thirties and the forties.

440. SWEENEY, JOHN L. "The Round Sunday Sounds," *New Republic*, 128 (April 6, 1953), 24–25. (Review of *Collected Poems*.)

441. TERRY, ARTHUR. "Dylan Thomas," *Rann*, No. 18 (March, 1953), 20–22. (Review of *Collected Poems*.)

442. TINDALL, WILLIAM YORK. "Burning and Crested Song," *American Scholar*, 22 (autumn, 1953), 486–90. (Review of *Collected Poems*.) An explicative review pointing out that, "with the possible exceptions of T. S. Eliot and Wallace Stevens, Thomas is the most excellent living poet in the English tongue."

443. WAIN, JOHN. *Mandrake*, 2 (summer and autumn, 1953), 261–63. (Review of *Collected Poems*.) A lengthy critical review of Thomas' poetical work listing both credit and debit sides of his work, perhaps a bit heavy on the latter.

### 1954

444. ANONYMOUS. "Obituary," *Wilson Library Bulletin*, 28 (January, 1954), 396.

445. ANONYMOUS. *Publishers' Weekly*, 165 (January 23, 1954), 333. Notes that New Directions has postponed publication of *Under Milk Wood* until a definitive version is chosen, at which time B.B.C. will perform the play; mentions one version being published in *Mademoiselle*, February, 1954. (*See* No. 204.)

446. ARROWSMITH, WILLIAM. "The Wisdom of Poetry," *Hudson Review*, 6 (winter, 1954), 597–604. (Review of *Collected Poems*.) A joint review of Thomas' work and the collected poems of Edwin Muir in which Thomas is considered second best. Arrowsmith feels that in Thomas "devotion to Process has resulted in a genuine truncation of the emotions or has forced him to artificialize his grief and his creatures so they can carry the intolerable weight of the life-process. Thomas is a primitive poet, and the cost of that primitive celebration is the loss of the civilized virtues and the problems of civilized men."

447. BRINNIN, JOHN MALCOLM. "Dylan Thomas and His Village," *Mademoiselle*, 38 (February, 1954), 108–9. An illustrated description of Laugharne and the pattern of a day in his Welsh village.

448. CANE, MELVILLE. "Are Poets Returning to Lyricism?" *Saturday Review*, 37 (January 16, 1954), 8–10+.

449. MUIR, EDWIN. "The Art of Dylan Thomas," *Harper's Bazaar*, 88 (February, 1954), 128–29.

450. OLSON, ELDER. "The Poetry of Dylan Thomas," *Poetry*, 83 (January, 1954), 213–20. (Review of *Collected Poems*.) A critical review of Thomas based on *Collected Poems*, having a broader scope and more explicative nature than the usual reviews of this work.

451. SITWELL, EDITH. "Dylan Thomas," *Atlantic Monthly*, 193 (February, 1954), 42–45.

## WORK IN PROGRESS ON THOMAS

452. STEARNS, MARSHALL W. *A Study*. Work in progress. Cornell University, 1949.

453. BLAINE, MARGARET L. *A Critical Study of the Prose and Poetry of Dylan Thomas*. Work in progress. University of Iowa, 1950.

454. KLEINMAN, HYMAN. *The Poetry of Thomas*. Work in progress. Columbia University, 1952.

## NOTES TO CHAPTER 1

### (*Pages 2–6*)

1. *The Collected Poems of Dylan Thomas* (Norfolk, Conn.: New Directions, 1953), p. 80. All citations of the poems are with reference to this volume, hereafter indicated as *CP*.

2. *Sunday Times* (London), 1936, as cited in Henry Treece, *Dylan Thomas* (London: Lindsay Drummond, 1949), p. 145.

3. Treece, *op. cit.*, p. 149.

4. While Freud states that "the relation between a symbol and the idea symbolized is an invariable one," it must be remarked that he uses "symbol" in a much narrower sense than his followers; he distinguishes four different relations which may exist "between dream-elements and the thoughts proper underlying them": substitution of part for whole, allusion, imagery, and symbolism. Notice the caveat in the following passage:

"If the symbols commonly appearing in dreams are well known, and also the personality of the dreamer, the conditions under which he lives, and the impressions in his mind after his dream occurred, we are often in a position to interpret it straightaway. . . . Such a feat flatters the vanity of the interpreter and impresses the dreamer. . . . But do not let this lead you astray; it is no part of our task to perform tricks, nor is that method of interpretation which is based on a knowledge of symbolism one which can replace, or even compare with, that of free association. It is complementary to this latter, and the results it yields are only useful when applied in connection with the latter" (*A General Introduction to Psychoanalysis,* trans. Joan Riviere [New York: Garden City Publishing Co., 1939], p. 135).

Observe also: "The symbolic relation is essentially that of a comparison, but not any kind of comparison. We must suspect that this comparison is subject to particular conditions, although we cannot say what these conditions are. Not everything with which an object or an occurrence can be compared appears in dreams as symbolic of it, and, on the other hand, dreams do not employ symbolism for anything and everything, but only for particular elements of latent dream-thoughts; there are thus limitations in both directions" (*ibid.,* p. 136).

Jung's views on the matter are most succinctly stated in his essay, "On the Relation of Analytical Psychology to Poetic Art," in *Contributions to Analytical Psychology,* trans. H. G. and Cary F. Baynes ("International Library of Psychology, Philosophy, and Scientific Method" [New York: Harcourt, Brace & Co., 1928]), pp. 225–49. I should like to call attention particularly to the following passages: "Only that aspect of art which consists in the process of artistic form can be an object of psychology; whereas that which constitutes the essential nature of art must always lie outside its province. This other aspect, namely, the problem what is art in itself, can never be the object of a psychological, but only of an aesthetico-artistic method of approach . . ." (p. 225). "If a work of art and a neurosis are explained in precisely similar terms, either the art-work must be a neurosis, or the neurosis a work of art. . . . A healthy human reason must assuredly revolt at the notion of art-work and neurosis being placed in the same category" (p. 227). "This kind of analysis brings the work of art into the sphere of general human psychology, whence everything else besides art may proceed. An explanation of a work of art obtained in this way is as great a futility as the statement that 'every artist is a narcissist'" (p. 229). "Because this kind of analysis is in no sense concerned with the art-work itself, but is always striving with the instinct of a mole to bury itself as quickly as possible in the murky background of the human psyche, it always finds itself in the same common earth that unites all mankind. Accordingly its explanations possess an indescribable monotony—that same tedious recital, in fact, which can daily be heard in certain medical consulting rooms" (p. 230). "[The psychologist considering a work of art must] adopt an exactly opposite attitude. . . . He will not raise the question, which for the art-work is quite superfluous, concerning its undoubted general antecedents, its basic human determinants; but he will inquire into the meaning of the work, and will be concerned with its preconditions only in so far as they are necessary for the understanding of its meaning . . ." (p. 233). "The art-work is not merely transmitted or derived—it is a creative organization of those very determinants to which a causalistic psychology must always reduce it. The plant is not a mere product of the soil; but a living creative process centred in itself, the essence of which has nothing to do with the character of the soil. In the same way the art-work must be regarded as a creative formation, freely making use of every precondition. Its meaning and its own individual particularity rests in itself, and not in its preconditions" (p. 234). After a division of art into two classes: "I would not, however, pledge myself to place the work of an unknown poet into either of these classes without previously having made a rather searching inquiry into the poet's personal relation to his work" (pp. 239–40). Note particularly the following: "The symbol is always a creation of an extremely complex nature, since data proceeding from every psychic function have entered into its composition" (*Psychological Types,* trans. H. Godwin Baynes ["International Library of Psychology, Philosophy, and Scientific Method" (New York: Harcourt, Brace & Co., 1926)], pp. 606–7).

For Jung the Freudian symbols are not symbols at all but signs or symptoms (*Contributions to Analytical Psychology,* pp. 231–32; *Psychological Types,* p. 606). Jung defines "symbol" as follows: "A conception which interprets the symbolic expression as the best possible formulation of a relatively unknown thing which cannot conceivably, therefore, be more clearly or characteristically represented is *symbolic"* (*ibid.*, p. 601). "The true symbol . . . should be understood as the expression of an intuitive perception which can as yet, neither be apprehended better, nor expressed differently" (*Contributions to Analytical Psychology*, p. 232).

The "symbolic" analysis which Jung is criticizing in most of these passages is the Freudian, which he repeatedly calls a "reductive method"; his own doctrine, of "primordial images" in the "collective unconscious," is put forward with many conditions and qualifications (see, e.g., *Psychological Types*, pp. 601, 603, 604, 605, and esp. pp. 554–60; also *Gestaltungen des Unbewussten* [Zurich: Rascher Verlag, 1950], pp. 5–11).

In its application to poetry, the doctrine amounts to the proposition that poetry is more effective as it is more universal; it is thus, in a sense, a psychological parallel to Aristotle's doctrine of τὸ καθόλου in poetry.

I cite these texts because they are the most readily available, but also because by that very fact they are works which anyone with even a minimal direct knowledge of the systems of Freud and Jung might be presumed to know.

5. This admission has been widely reported—it appears even on the dust jacket of the *Collected Poems;* but I have been unable to locate it. Perhaps it was made orally; if the remarks made in answer to an inquiry by Geoffrey Grigson (*New Verse*, No. 11, October, 1934, pp. 8–9) are intended, they are very far from any such admission. Thomas' words are: "It [poetry] must drag further into the clean nakedness of light more even of the hidden causes than Freud could realize."

6. *CP*, p. 6.

7. E.g., *CP*, pp. 35, 41–44, 49–50, 54–55, 63, 65, 78–79.

8. *CP*, p. 63.

9. See below, p. 87.

10. "The Map of Love," in *The Map of Love: Verse and Prose* (London: J. M. Dent & Sons, Ltd., 1939), p. 64.

11. For a discussion of symbolism as it is conceived in this volume see my "Dialogue on Symbolism," in *Critics and Criticism*, ed. Ronald S. Crane (Chicago: University of Chicago Press, 1952),

esp. pp. 581–87. A much broader and fuller treatment of the subject can be found in Richard P. McKeon's brilliant essay, "Symbols, Myths, and Arguments," originally delivered as a paper at the Thirteenth Conference on Science, Philosophy, and Religion and soon to be published in *Symbols and Values: An Initial Study,* ed. Lyman Bryson *et al.* (New York: Harper & Bros., 1954).

12. See below, p. 15.

13. *CP,* p. 5.

14. *CP,* p. 144.

15. *CP,* p. xv.

16. *CP,* p. 27.

17. *CP,* p. 110.

18. *CP,* p. 108.

19. *CP,* p. 29.

20. *CP,* p. 41.

21. *CP,* p. 4.

22. *CP,* p. 158.

23. I intend by the terms "sentimental" and "romantic," in this passage, the debased or sensational kinds; for example, the cheaply pathetic soap opera and the ordinary magazine love story.

## NOTES TO CHAPTER 2
### (*Pages 19–20*)

1. *New Verse,* October, 1934. Cited in Henry Treece, *Dylan Thomas* (London: Lindsay Drummond, 1949), p. 39.

2. *CP,* p. 159.

3. I take the first period as covering the contents of *Eighteen Poems* and *Twenty-five Poems,* represented by the first eighty-five pages of the *Collected Poems;* the second as covering the contents of *The Map of Love* and *Deaths and Entrances* (excepting from the latter "Poem in October," "Into her Lying Down Head," "A Winter's Tale," "Vision and Prayer," the "Ballad of the Long-legged Bait," "Holy Spring," and "Fern Hill," which seem to me to initiate the final period). The second period spans, with these exceptions, pp. 86–180 of the *Collected Poems,* and the third includes the remainder. All this is mere approximation; the close reader of Dylan Thomas will see what I mean by it. I hope it is

clear that I think there are magnificent poems in each of these periods; I should be very sorry to see my remarks interpreted as constituting a history either of poetic progress or of poetic regress, for my purpose is merely to differentiate what is obviously different.

4. Treece, *op. cit.*, pp. 159 and 135.

5. *CP*, p. 112.

6. *CP*, p. 152.

7. *CP*, p. 168.

8. *CP*, p. 56.

9. *CP*, p. 152.

## NOTES TO CHAPTER 3
### (*Pages 33–40*)

1. *New Verse*, October, 1934.

2. Cited in Henry Treece, *Dylan Thomas* (London: Lindsay Drummond, 1949), p. 47, n.1.

3. See, e.g., Kenneth Rexroth, *The New British Poets* (Norfolk, Conn.: New Directions, n.d. [1949]), pp. xvii ff.

4. *CP*, p. 14.

5. *CP*, p. 15.

6. *CP*, p. 17.

7. *CP*, p. 34.

8. *CP*, p. 70.

## NOTES TO CHAPTER 4
### (*Page 46*)

1. "Salute to a Poet," *Times Literary Supplement* (London), October 28, 1952, p. 776.

2. Henry Treece, *Dylan Thomas* (London: Lindsay Drummond, 1949), p. 141.

## NOTES TO CHAPTER 5
### (*Pages 55–58*)

1. Henry Treece, *Dylan Thomas* (London: Lindsay Drummond, 1949), p. 149.

2. *CP*, pp. 84, 21, 22, 171, 150, respectively.

3. *CP*, p. 80.
4. *CP*, pp. 179 and 113.
5. *CP*, pp. 179 and 132.
6. *CP*, pp. 80, 112, 147.
7. *CP*, pp. 42–43.
8. *CP*, p. 62.
9. *CP*, pp. 19 and 69.
10. *CP*, p. 35.
11. *CP*, p. 172.
12. *CP*, p. 22.

## NOTES TO CHAPTER 6
### (*Pages 64–65*)

1. Thus Marshall W. Stearns, whose essay, "Unsex the Skeleton" (*Sewanee Review*, LII [summer, 1944], 424–40), remains one of the more serious efforts to understand Thomas, speaks of the sonnets as a "loosely-connected" series and proceeds on that view to treat Sonnet VIII by itself. The sequence was published bit by bit in magazines but was referred to as a work in progress; and even though Sonnets IX and X alone appear in the *Selected Writings* (New York: New Directions, 1939), I hope that the ensuing discussion will show the sequence to be a single poem.

2. See above, p. 8.

3. The general view of myth as an oblique expression of knowledge is of course very ancient and has had a continuous history of support. See, e.g., Plato *Phaedrus* 229; Cicero *De natura deorum* ii. xxiv ff.; Plutarch *De Iside et Osiride* xx. lviii; and, to pass over medieval examples, which are legion, Sir Francis Bacon, *The Wisdom of the Ancients*, Preface.

4. See Charles Anthon, *A Dictionary of Classical Antiquities* (New York, 1867), p. 599, col. 2, for these and further references, and indeed for a discussion of the whole question. I confess some doubt about Anthon's presentation of the case: first, because he is very free in his manipulation of the twelve labors and, second, because I wonder about the authority, in this matter, of writers so late as Plutarch (b. A.D. 46), Porphyry (b. A.D. 233), and the authors of the "Orphic Hymns," few of which, by general con-

sent, can be much earlier than A.D. 350. I think this, in short, a case where the inherent probability of the position is greater than that of the evidence which can be marshaled in its favor, and should prefer to leave it at that, for the argument merely from consistent interpretation is full of danger and tends to prove the ingenuity of the interpreter rather than the historical fact. Those who wish to see a particularly hideous example of this argument, on this particular subject, may read Arthur Drews, *Der Sternhimmel in der Dichtung und Religion der alten Völker und des Christentums* (Jena, 1923); Drews reduces to constellational myth not merely the Greek, Persian, Jewish, etc., religions, but the Gospels of Mark and Matthew and the Revelations according to St. John.

The real point here, of course, is not the historic fact but the possibility that the poet may have known and used the tradition. I think there is excellent reason to suppose that he used, among other sources, a popular work on astronomy likely to be found in most old-fashioned private libraries: Mrs. Norman Lockyer's translation of Camille Flammarion, *The Wonders of the Heavens* ("Humboldt Library of Popular Science Literature," Vol. I, No. 14). Flammarion here not merely touches on many points which enter into the essential design of the sonnets but, remarking that Francœur had maintained the view just mentioned, proceeds to a detailed exposition of the Herculean labors in astronomical terms (p. 74, cols. 2 ff.).

5. It should be said that pagan antiquity did not call the constellation "Hercules." In the earliest Greek astronomical treatise extant, the *Phainomena* of Aratus (b. *ca.* 315 B.C.), the figure is called "Engonasin" ("On His Knees"), "Gnyx" ("The Kneeler"), or "Eidolon" ("Ghost," "Phantom," "Image"). Similarly, Latin poets call it "Nixus," "Effigies," "Imago." In the *Almagest* Ptolemy gives τοῦ ἐγγόνασιν ἀστερισμός. The name "Hercules Ingeniculus" is thought to have been first applied to it by Avienus (*fl.* A.D. 366); however, "Many MSS. of Germanicus actually represent Engonasin as Hercules," according to G. R. Mair (*Callimachus, Lycophron, and Aratus* ["Loeb Classical Library" (London, 1931)], p. 373). Aratus treats the sign as representing a toiler at a mysterious task: "That sign no one knows how to read clearly, nor on what task he is bent" (trans. Mair); Cicero, closely

following Aratus, in *De natura deorum* ii. xlii adds the epithets "weary" and "sorrowing": "Attingens defessa velut maerentis imago / Vertitur. . . ."

6. *Op. cit.*, p. 66, col. 2. Charles Everitt ("Constellation," *Encyclopædia Britannica* [11th ed.], VII, 13) makes the same ascription, probably on the authority of Flammarion. I can find no record of any such work by Bede and have no idea what text may be referred to.

7. Flammarion, *op. cit.*, p. 66, col. 2. In his *Popular Astronomy,* trans. J. Ellard Gore (New York: D. Appleton & Co., n.d.), p. 375, Flammarion reports his possession of an illuminated folio of 1661 which represents "the sky delivered from pagans and peopled with Christians." The most thoroughgoing effort to Christianize the heavens, according to Flammarion, was the *Coelum stellatum Christianum* of Julius Schiller (1627), which peopled the sky with saints, apostles, popes, bishops, etc. Earlier attempts at this sort of thing, so far as I can learn, were sporadic and timid, although there are traces of attempts in the thirteenth century to name the planets after angels (e.g., Peter of Abano *Conciliator* Diff. 9 [see Thorndike, *History of Magic and Experimental Science* (New York, 1923), II, 900]), and Virgo had been made into the Virgin Mary even earlier by Albumazar (see Hermann of Carinthia, *De essentiis,* ed. P. Manuel Alonso [Comillas, 1946], pp. 29–30, and the *Speculum astronomicum* ascribed to Albertus Magnus, ed. Borgnet, X, 644).

8. For Abaddon see Rev. 9:11. In the *Evangelium Bartholomei* he is made into Death himself. As to "atlas-eater," the constellation Boötes was sometimes identified with Atlas, because the celestial pole formerly lay close to it; there is also a star Atlas in Pleiades (f Tauri or Pleiadum, R.A. 3$^h$ 45$^m$, Decl. N. 23° 51'); but I doubt whether there is any reference to either the constellation or the star.

9. Lilius Gyraldus, *De deis gentium varia et multiplex historia* (Basel, 1548), Syntagma VI: "Pluto, et caeteri inferorum dei," p. 266A: "Tricerberum vero canem eius [i.e., Plutonis] subjiciebant pedibus quod mortalium iurgiorum invidiae ternario conflentur statu, id est, naturali, casuali, & accidentali, ut Fulgentij ipsius verbis utar. Alij vero sic tradunt . . . canis autem, frugum a terra partium tripartito, in proiectionem arationem & germinationem

dividi, notabat." Also p. 296A: "Cerberus dictus quasi κρεόβορος, hoc est carnem vorans." Matthias Martinus, *Lexicon philologicum,* holds to the same etymology a century later and adds: "ut significetur terra, quae mortua corpora consumit." According to Isidore of Seville xi. 3.33, the three heads signify "tres aetates per quas mors hominem devorat, id est infantiam, iuventutem, senectutem." See also H. Theodore Silverstein, *Dante and Vergil the Mystic* ("Harvard Studies and Notes in Philology and Literature," Vol. XIV [Cambridge, 1932]), pp. 61–62 and notes. Natalis Comes (*Mythologia,* Lib. viii, c. xiii, p. 457, col. 2) lists among the names of the Great Dog the name "Proöphagus," or "one who eats early."

The connection between Cerberus and Canis Major is given by Flammarion in the work I have already suggested as one of Thomas' sources: "Well-known authors even think that . . . he was Cerberus. . . . Their opinion is supported by this coincidence, that the Great Dog guards at the equator the lower hemisphere of the Egyptians, in the same manner as Cerberus watched the region of Tartarus." (Flammarion evidently does not credit this view and insists on the long and honorable history of Sirius.)

10. The sun is frequently compared to a cock by Thomas, e.g., "suncock" (*CP,* p. 64). "Heaven's egg" is a reference to the ancient notion of the Cosmic Egg, common enough in both Eastern and Western thought; see, e.g., the *Khandogya-Upanishad,* Nineteenth Khanda, 1–4, and Guillaume de Conches *De philos. mundi* iv. i (ed. Migne, XC, 1167C, and CLXXII, 84A).

11. See the "Bohn Library" translation of Plutarch's *Moralia* (by C. W. King), *Theosophical Essays,* p. 146.

12. These curious notions about the pelican are first found in the *Physiologus.* According to Isidore *Etymologiae* xii. 7. 26, "Pellicanus avis Aegyptia habitans in solitudine Nili fluminis. . . . Fertur, si verum est, eam occidere natos suos, eosque per triduum lugere, deinde se ipsam vulnerare et aspersione sui sanguinis vivificare filios." The analogy to the immolation of Christ is obvious, and the pelican was early accepted as a Christian symbol. See, e.g., Dante, *Paradiso,* XXV, 112 ff., and Drummond's sonnet "For the Passion," in *Flowers of Sion* ("Muses' Library," Vol. II), p. 11.

13. Cf. Dante, *Paradiso,* XVIII, 13–42, esp. 16–38. God is here called "la favilla pura," or "the pure spark," but the attributes

dealt with are identical with those questioned in Sonnet IV. Dante's source is Aristotle *Metaphysics* 1072$^b$3–1073$^a$13. Thomas also speaks of God as a spark in *CP*, p. 27.

14. This tradition has been transmitted to us by Dante, among others; see *Inferno*, I, 38.

15. The doctrine of the sexual seduction of Eve by the Serpent is rabbinical in origin and based on Gen. 5:3. Isaac de Beausobre (*Histoire de Manichée et du manichéisme* [Amsterdam, 1739], Vol. II, Book VI, ix, p. 409) cites Pirk, the *Apothegmata* of Rabbi Eliezer: "Accessit ad Evam Serpens, atque gravida facta est ex Caïno."

16. Measuring from "the first point of Aries," the sun is at 270° at its farthest point south of the Equator, "close" to M8 in Sagittarius, which is R.A. 18$^h$ 1$^m$, Decl. S. 24°. Since the sun thus "dies" at 270° and is "born" at a point immediately after, the "marrow-ladle / Out of the wrinkled undertaker's van" may mean "life out of death" simply. The van may also refer to Ophiucus, particularly Serpens Cauda, but Delphinus ("Job's Coffin") is more probable. The ladle is pretty clearly Sagittarius, the "Milk-Dipper." The sun in fact enters the further branch of the Milky Way somewhat before 270° and remains in it until "weaned" at about 282°.

17. Compare "sad stride of autumn and winter shuffle," "The Mouse and the Woman," sec. 18, in *Selected Writings*, p. 135.

18. "Button" is also used as a symbol of denial in "One Warm Saturday," in *Selected Writings*, p. 162.

19. *CP*, p. 131.

20. Thomas may also have had in mind the present drift of the earth toward Lyra. This led to the popular misconception, much stimulated by the more sensational press some years ago, that the earth might eventually be destroyed by collision with Lyra. Thus the term "sirens" would have its basis in the analogy, song of the sirens : a ship :: the "music" of the Lyre : earth. See the first sonnet of Edna St. Vincent Millay's "Epitaph for the Race of Man," in *Wine from These Grapes* (New York: Harper & Bros., 1934), p. 57, where the notion is used, and indeed given this very treatment.

21. In this connection a passage from Aldous Huxley's *Antic Hay* is of some interest: "But time passed, time passed flowing in a dark

stream, as though from some profound wound in the world's side, bleeding, bleeding forever" (chap. xiii). The use of wax as a symbol for mortal or dead flesh is frequent in Thomas; oil is sometimes set against it as a symbol of life. See "oil of life" ("The Mouse and the Woman," sec. 8, in *Selected Writings*, p. 129); "the secret oils that drive the grass" (*CP*, p. 27); "turns [my blood] to wax" (*CP*, p. 10); "oil of tears" (*CP*, p. 29).

22. Observe that Libra is "the scaled sea-sawers" also because (1) it is the Scales; (2) the sea-signs have deluged it, brought about its setting; (3) scales "see-saw"; (4) "see-saw" as a word contains the present and past tenses of the verb "see," hence contains an implicit allusion to time. Note, too, how a pun on "scales" easily makes the "sea-sawers" into scaled monsters.

23. The rainbow is very commonly depicted as "three-colored" in medieval illuminations; for example, the rainbow above Noah's Ark in a Norman Book of Hours executed about 1430 (Bodleian Library, MS Auct. D inf. 2. II, fol. 59ᵛ). The conception of the bow as so colored appears twice in *Paradise Lost* (XI, 865–66 and 897) and earlier in Drummond, Sylvester, and Du Bartas, whom Sylvester translated. The conception is peripatetic, having its origin in Aristotle *Meteorologica* iii. iii. 371ᵇ34 ff. A rainbow is modernly thought of as having seven colors—red, orange, yellow, green, blue, indigo, and violet. Aristotle seems to have grouped together the first three, as well as the last three, thus producing a three-colored bow. If Thomas is being even more precise, Deneb and Albireo (Alpha and Beta Cygni, respectively) would give three colors, for Albireo is a double, a golden third-magnitude star attended by a fifth-magnitude blue star at a distance of 35″; they are, however, respectively, at the head and the foot of the Cross. In fact, the Milky Way itself divides above the head of the Cross and passes through the *extremities* of its arms, not through the "nipples" of Christ.

24. Of course the constellation Triangulum is also in the sky at this time; and Andromeda was renamed the Holy Sepulcher.

25. *CP*, p. 72.

26. "The Mouse and the Woman," sec. 18, in *Selected Writings*, p. 135.

27. Argo was not wrecked, although in the Symplegades or

Clashing Islands, the *corymbi,* or stern ornaments, were sheared off (see Valerius Flaccus *Argonautica* iv. 692, or Apollonius Rhodius *Argonautica* ii. 601–2). The constellation Argo Navis was divided by modern astronomers because its hugeness made it inconvenient for reference; perhaps it is this, and the fact that its parts are widely scattered, that makes Thomas think of it as "wrecked" or "racked"—his word being of course a pun on the old form "wracked."

28. It appears first in the catalogue of Nicholas Louis de Lacaille, published posthumously in 1769.

29. "Bible east," i.e., from the direction of the Holy Land, or southeast.

30. Aquila appears to be "Christ's Eagle"; see Rev. 4:7 and Dante, *Purgatorio,* XXIX, 88 ff., *Paradiso,* XXVI, 52. Thomas may be playing on the notion that the eagle is sacred to the sun (Son). The notion of the eagle as foreseeing and foretelling is "druidical"; according to a book which I should say Thomas quite certainly knew, Edward Davies' *The Mythology and Rites of the British Druids* (London, 1809), pp. 163–64, "The Welsh romantic chronicles of the fourteenth century inform us that this lake [Lomond] . . . contains sixty islands, each of which has a *rock* or *petra,* with an eagle's nest on its top—that these eagles assemble annually at a central *petra,* on May-day, and by their concert of screams, vaticinate the fates of countries and kingdoms for the ensuing year." See also p. 162 of Davies for the rock as a symbol of the "harbour of life."

31. See Rev. 22:1–2 for the River, which is evidently identical with that of Eden (Gen. 2:10); the Tree of Life is also mentioned, and there is thus some presumption that the Garden itself is restored in the New Jerusalem.

32. I should say "one of the passages," for the Harrowing is more commonly traced to the apocryphal *Evangelium Nicodemi,* or the third-century *Descensus Christi ad inferos,* which was subsequently combined with the *Gesta Pilati.* "Peter" doubtless also refers to Aries, for that constellation was renamed "St. Peter" by Christian astronomers and astrologists; it is fairly "near" the Milky Way, earlier treated as a rainbow, and, as the first sign of spring, is first to greet the resurrected sun.

33. See Rev. 22:16: "I am the root. . . ." Cf. Zech. 6:12.

34. The "two bark towers" are the Tree of Knowledge and the Tree of Life (Gen. 2:9). Observe that Thomas suggests that the Garden will be restored and that the Serpent will participate in its restoration as in its loss, thus bringing to an end Time, Death, and other consequences of the Fall. It would seem almost as though he is adopting the old doctrine of *apokatastasis,* which came out of a Stoic treatment of the Magnus Annus and was developed by Origenists and Cerinthians to mean the eventual redemption of the devil himself. St. Augustine writes (*De haeres. haer.* c. 43) that the Origenists thought that "etiam diabolos cum omnibus damnatis spem habere liberationis ex infero." See also *Contra Julianum* v. xlvii and vi. x.

The mass of somewhat recondite information contained in the sonnets and other poems of Thomas did not, in all likelihood, come from any of the original sources. He undoubtedly read popular works and *occulta;* besides Flammarion and Davies, he must have been acquainted with such books as Lewis Spence's volumes on Atlantis, his *The Mysteries of Britain,* and his *Encyclopaedia of Occultism;* and with the "Bohn Library" volumes of Ennemoser's *History of Magic, The Encyclopaedia of Occultism,* Hind's *Introduction to Astronomy,* and Lilly's *Introduction to Astrology.* His many astronomical references, and his curious fondness for Atlas, suggest that he at one time or another read a good deal of Drummond of Hawthornden, who, like Donne, would have been a mine of Christian tradition for him. I have indicated remoter sources in these notes merely to assist the student of Thomas to run down the poet's more immediate ones.

By a curious accident, I happened to read Blake a few days after I had completed this book, and was struck at once by the constellational symbolism of the symbolic and didactic works. On looking into the matter, I found that this aspect of Blake's symbolism had already been dealt with, very ably indeed, by Milton O. Percival in *William Blake's Circle of Destiny* (New York: Columbia University Press, 1938), chap. viii. The resemblance between Blake and Thomas, so far as symbolism is concerned, is so remarkable that it deserves some considerable study.

35. "Day" is a reference to Rev. 22:5: "And there shall be

no more curse"; perhaps the metaphor of a nest comes from *Paradiso*, XVIII, 110–11: "e da lui si rammenta / quella virtù ch'è forma per li nidi." The "worm" is of course the Serpent, as in Sonnet III. The reference in a "rainbow's quayrail" is to Rev. 4:2–6. Revelations seems to be heavily involved in this last sonnet, quite appropriately for a poem which is the Apocalypse of the heavens, in which "the heavens declare the glory of God."

36. "The Mouse and the Woman," sec. 22, in *Selected Writings*, p. 136.

# INDEX OF POEMS CITED

[The references in this index are to pages in the book, exclusive of the Bibliography, on which individual poems of Thomas are discussed, quoted from, or otherwise alluded to. The titles appear as in the Contents of *The Collected Poems of Dylan Thomas* (1953).]

[ PRINTED IN U·S·A ]